T0121961

# CHANGING CHAPTERS

*A Sister's Story*

CLARA JOBSON

**BALBOA.**
PRESS

A DIVISION OF HAY HOUSE

Balboa Press books may be ordered through booksellers or by contacting:

Balboa Press
A Division of Hay House
1663 Liberty Drive
Bloomington, IN 47403
www.balboapress.com.au
1 (877) 407-4847

ISBN: 978-1-4525-2700-0 (sc)
ISBN: 978-1-4525-2701-7 (e)

Printed in the United States of America.

Balboa Press rev. date: 01/08/2015

To my children and my family

A past hidden is a future lost,
But turning the page is only the beginning.

# CONTENTS

# PREFACE

Life. Isn't it a bitch? One moment you can be on top of the world, the next, *smash*, into the ground you go. We are all the same in many ways. Some people have been broken, some have been pushed to their limit, some have had their very souls compromised. We often see others who have no sadness or tragedy in their lives … or at least that is what we are led to believe. We never see what lies beneath their stories.

Each of us has his or her own life journey. This is my journey, my road, my story. People often doubt the truth because it is horrifying. They don't want to admit that the unimaginable has happened and continues to happen. Facing evil can divide a country as well a family.

My brother's own journey was filled with pain, anger, and self-destruction. His name was James Jobson, or Big Jim as he was called during his bikie years. James was seventeen years old when the bikie world drew him in. During his many years with the two bikie clubs, he did terrible things to many people at the request of the club presidents and their councils—things I am sure he later regretted. There were car bombings, shop bombings, murders, drugs, turf wars, and brothels. Breaking the law was all a game.

After many years of living a life that was not good, James found his road becoming clearer. I have no love for the people who played various roles in his life. I believe he was betrayed. He trusted the wrong people, and in the end, it was an enemy disguised as a friend who came back to haunt him and eventually took his life.

Pain has also been a part of my journey, but on a different level. My childhood was steeped in violence, rape, and molestation. Sadly, I walk this road with many other children. I ask you to open your heart and mind and, before passing final judgment, look behind the masks that people wear. If presented with the same set of circumstances, which path would you have chosen?

Other people's lives can directly affect our own. Within personal tragedy or even triumph, we all have the ability to alter the chapters of our lives. I personally believe that these chapters are mapped out long before we are born, and in believing this, I know that no matter how hard our lives seem or have been, the chapters themselves are not set in concrete. Our life paths are there for us to follow and experience. Whether we have the ability to choose which direction is the right one is still a mystery. They say God only gives us what we can handle, but it's through free will that evil is committed. I believe that God gives us the tools to see our way through the evil.

It is possible to change direction in a blinding flash. My story is about betrayal, survival, tragedy, and triumph, and this follows the lives of my brother and I. This is our story. I am not saying our lives are any more extraordinary than anyone else's, but ours is the story that I want to tell.

It is a story of surviving a childhood from hell. It's about witnessing domestic violence at the highest level and what effect it had on us. Sexual abuse was something we both experienced. We were brought up in a household full of secrets, lies, and deceit. It was a terrible start for any young child, but it was the beginning of a lifetime of extraordinary events for both of us.

*Changing Chapters* is not only about my brother's life with two bikie clubs, Satan's Sons and Devil's Dogs; it's also about finding the courage and strength to change the path you were destined for. Even with so many backward steps at the start, there is proof that one can succeed in changing midway. I suppose it is also therapy for me. Being able to write about the most horrific things in your life is like being released from pain, guilt, and regrets. Most of all, it is about being able to say, "I'm not a victim anymore."

I am a survivor with hope and a new direction. There have been many backward steps taken into what had become my comfort zone. Stepping forward meant going somewhere I hadn't been before, a pretty scary place. Yet it was a place where I could feel safe in body and in mind. My brother's life ended in an instant and was filled with great pain. A real shame, because I believe he was robbed of a great conclusion.

I have written this book in the hope of setting the record straight. There have been many things written about my brother—some true, but some that are so wrong it's actually criminal. The media and newspapers really only print or record what they want people to know, or what sells papers. I would love for our full story to be told. I hope that people who think that the criminal or bikie world is the only way will maybe see it differently after reading this book. I believe that no matter what happens in our lives, we all have free will to be better people. We need conviction, and this is what I have.

I am the best person to write our story and the story of my brother's life in the bikie world because I was there and lived this pain.

*Success is not final, failure is not fatal:*
*it is the courage to continue that counts.*
*—Winston Churchill*

# PART ONE

## *Childhood Pathways*

# CHAPTER 1

## *Domestic Violence*

A person who thinks he or she has the right to hurt another person or persons has the unsettling ability to place blame and fault with the victim. Where is the logic? Where do such individuals find justification for their terrible actions? Sadly, they do. Are these good men doing bad things? Do they know what they do or what they want? Disbelieving that they are to blame, they blind themselves with lies to cover the truth. They feel no guilt, no shame—nothing.

Sadly, their victims feel all of the above. Those of us who live through these terrible events often come out the other side damaged. So with that, I'll start my journey through my life in our world of domestic violence. Evil is not only committed by the offender but also by people who stand by and do nothing.

It was a warm and balmy day in our hometown. Nothing really extraordinary was happening. I was on my way to visit the counsellor I had seen a couple of times since my doctor had sent me to her. I was suffering from depression and anxiety. I was also about five months pregnant with my son. I had recently left my children's father after he slapped me across the face during a stupid argument.

I have never liked violence, especially against women and children. I witnessed horrible domestic violence as a child, and I was never going to go through that myself or put my children in that same situation. I used to have terrible nightmares when I was young and was always a very nervous child. I'm not really sure whether the violence or the sexual abuse I suffered was the cause. There was a very fine line between the two.

One of my greatest problems was that I never slept well. Restlessness and bad dreams kept me from sleeping through the night. I didn't really think that it was insomnia, because mine was a behaviour learned over many years. Whilst we were at home, my brother and I never slept well. We had to be on guard in case my father came home drunk or angry. I was always in this sort of hazy sleep. If I was at my auntie and uncle's house, I was always wondering whether my uncle would sleaze his way into my room. But that's another chapter.

As I sat in the counsellor's office waiting for my name to be called, my memory was going wild. *Where do I start with this session? Fuck.* My life always seemed to be in a mess. I just wanted to have a great life with my kids and partner, but he fucked that up when he hit me. I kept thinking, *God, it was only a small slap. Why have I reacted this way?* As I sat there waiting, watching my little girl play with some blocks, memories came flooding back of the screams of terror and tears that never stopped. My heart raced as I recalled the hideous things my father put all of us through.

I can honestly say I can't remember the first time I saw my father beat my mother. My memories are all over the place; they jump from one moment in time to the next. I don't know why. Maybe the events I can recall were not the worst of it. Maybe my mind has to lock some of them away as a survival mechanism.

My name was called. As I stood, Gay, my counsellor, approached me. I told my young daughter, "Time for you to go and see Fee." Fee was the childcare lady at the clinic. She was a very pleasant lady, very chatty and polite. She always had a smile when she greeted me. She wasn't much taller than I and maybe a little overweight. She had a warmth about her that made me feel safe.

Gay and I made small talk as we walked to her office. "How are you?" she asked.

"Good," I replied.

"How is your daughter?"

"Good."

"And the baby?"

"Yeah, doing well."

When we reached her office, I scanned to see if there was anything new. Gay asked if there was anything bothering me.

"Um, yeah. Where to start. The dreams and nightmares are all so real, but what I'm trying to work out is whether that was why I left my children's father. Do you think it was about the slap?"

"No," Gay said. "I think it was about women and violence. You've told me you feel uncomfortable about men hitting women."

"Yeah, I told him he would only ever do it once." I started to tell her about a time when I was small and my father hurt my mum. It was like my mind was a computer, sifting through moments.

At the same time as I was seeing Gay, I was also seeing a psychologist named Dick. He was a good man, a gentle soul, and he helped me believe there were good men out there. He was steady and quiet in his approach and gentle in his tone of voice. Dick was a middle-aged man with glasses, greying hair, and a beard.

Dick helped me to sleep. He hypnotized me a few times. I recall the first time as if it were yesterday. We were in his office. His office was a lot different from Gay's. Her office was neat and orderly—how I would have my office. Dick's was messy, with stuff all over the place. But it had a warmth about it.

He told me to relax as much as I could. We talked about my brother and me as children. He asked me to think about the last time I felt safe.

I remembered it as he talked to me. My mind started the long journey back, and I recalled playing with James in our backyard. I could see I was safe there. It was soothing in a way. My body felt calm, and I could not recall the last time I felt that way—being kids and being free.

James was laughing and playing in the sand. I was pretending to be a singer and dancer. The memory brought a momentary smile to my face because we were safe. I used to love pretending I was a famous singer. I had awesome moves. Well, I thought I did. James would roll around and laugh at me.

But then I felt a great sadness. It took over the whole moment. I felt a tightness across my chest, like I was being restrained somehow. There was no freedom in my actions, and I was becoming anxious. Dick brought me back to the present, his voice softly whispering my name and reassuring me that I was safe. As I came back into the moment. I sighed. Reality can be a terrible thing when it represents sorrow and sadness.

Tears were rolling down my face, and I was visibly shaken. Dick asked in his gentle voice, "Where did you go?" I told him about the memory of James and I playing. I had to go back thirty-six years to find a place where I was safe. I really did not want to leave that moment. It was like sitting in a warm bath, submerged in a feeling of utter peace. It was obviously the last time I felt safe and the beginning of being afraid.

For a small child, this a terrifying place. There is no exit or pause button; it is just what goes on every day. Being afraid becomes part of who you are. But being afraid can lead to great courage.

As James and I grew up, a silent truth bonded us. I've always imagined this played a huge part in who I am, as I am always busy, always moving, maybe too scared to stop. Our father had a split personality. Well, at least I hope that's what it was. Otherwise, he was just pure evil. We came to hate this man for many years. James never really forgave him; I tried.

I'm not saying all the memories of our father are bad, but unfortunately, the bad ones take precedence. They are the ones that have haunted me and my brother all the days of our lives. They're the ones that helped forge the steps we took as people.

This chapter is about the terror we were exposed to. I know many people have also lived this terrible shame, and we all have a sad story to tell. Our stories are our truths. I hope reading my family's story may help other souls who have lost their way. I have made my journey to this point and survived. Unfortunately, my brother didn't.

The assaults on our mother were so bad that when other people recall these events, it is like something out of a horror story. People watch but think, *Surely this can't be true.* People often asked me if it was the truth, and they would be in total shock when I told them it was. What they had heard was so unbelievable. We learned to hide the truth. This was the start of how we were taught to lie.

Our father beat our mother with so much anger. I used to wonder, *What happened to this man to make him so angry with his wife and children? What has Mum done?* I tried to remember, but nothing came to mind. As children, you think the simplest things. We used to make sure we didn't upset him or make him angry so that we wouldn't get hurt that way. But he could be drunk or sober, and it didn't really matter. It was as if we didn't know the man standing in front of us. He became someone else, someone we really did not like.

As young kids, we could do nothing but scream and in fear. We tried to get between our parents, doing anything to try to stop it, our hearts pounding and our faces screwed up with fear and wet with tears. There just did not seem to be a pattern to his attacks. The events that I recall are the ones that have been embedded in my head and my memories.

Often when I remember some terrible event, it's like living a horror story in which we all had the starring roles. My earliest memories go back to when I was very young. We were living in a state house in a tree-lined suburb. Our father didn't really ever have a steady job. He would do odd jobs, and he also trained a couple of horses. I remember he was always looking for an easy way out

The house was quite small. It had three small bedrooms, one bathroom, and one toilet. The laundry was on the back veranda. The yards in this neighbourhood were larger. Kids could play and were safe in their own yards. But not us. Our father had some despicable and dreadful friends he would bring to the house. He always seemed to be drawn to people with no morals, people you really would not turn your back on, let alone bring into your home.

I recall an evening when were we were at home and our father was out with one of his undesirable brothers-in-law. It must have been early evening, as we were still awake with Mum. Our father came running into the house screaming at Mum; I'm not really sure why. I remember Mum grabbing James and me very quickly and laying us down in front of the fireplace. She lay over us as a noise went off that I had never heard before. It was so frightening. Our windows shattered as bullets were fired into our front lounge room.

It seemed our father and his relative had an argument so bad the other man went home and got a gun. As we lay there in fear, not really sure if we were going to live or die at the hands of another madman, our father was yelling at Mum. I don't remember why. I think I was paralysed with fear.

Mum was shocked at the episode that had just unfolded. James and I thought, *Jeez, I really don't want to make him angry. Imagine what he would do to us!* Well, *I* thought that. James was only a small toddler.

As our father's relative drove off, our father got himself up. I remember the broken glass being shattered all over the floor and bullet holes in our house. As she stood up, Mum whispered to me, "Watch your brother."

Then, as if things weren't already bad enough, our father ran at Mum, grabbing her by the hair. This was a trick of his to gain total power. She was screaming and yelling, as he was now punching her and kicking her like she was some sort of animal. I remember screaming and holding James, as he was just a little boy.

The terror just seemed to go on and on, with blood now pouring out of her. He kept it up, kicking, punching, saying terrible things to her. It was terrifying. Not only had our house been shot up, but now this.

James kept trying to get in between them. This was like a game that we would never win. Our father would grip onto her hair even tighter, with his knees now in her face. It would seem to last forever. I don't know how long the attack went on, for there never seemed to be any great length. Finally he stopped as Mum fell to the ground.

James went and clung to her. She was lying so still, no movement. Maybe she was dead. I yelled at our father, telling him, "You have killed her!" He locked himself into the bedroom and left us, traumatized and not knowing what to do, two small children just clinging to their mum and each other.

Mum finally moved and slowly picked herself up—covered in blood, in pain, and with an overwhelming feeling of shame and guilt. She cuddled James and me and told us she would be okay, that we would always be together. Finally she made her way into the bathroom to clean up. We sat in our room, and because it was close to the bathroom, we could see her face with blood all over, smearing as it hit the tears on her face.

Later, she came into our room to put us to bed. We got down on our small bent knees with our eyes closed and hands joined together to say our prayers. "Dear God," I prayed, "please keep Mummy and baby James safe, and please God, help our dad not be so mean and bad to us." I used to think God must be so busy, because he hadn't answered my prayers. Maybe we needed to pray more so he'd hear us whilst we lived.

We lay there afterward listening for any movement from him, but usually, if he went to bed, he went to sleep. I lay there chewing my fingernails and fidgeting. We listened to our mum cry in pain and shame as she slowly cleaned the mess up. We heard her pick up the broom and sweep all the glass, and then scoop it up and put it in the bin. We had no windows at the front of the house now, as they had all been smashed, so she hung up blankets to hide the inside of the house. Our house was always the talking point of the street.

The assaults were kept from Mum's family. Week after week, the bashings continued. If Mum wasn't black and blue, we would be able to visit our cousins or go to see Nana and Pops.

My schoolwork was constantly under strain. I would go to school with a low heart, not knowing whether she would be okay. Would she be alive when I got back? What about James, would he be okay? I started to think of myself as the main protector of James. I would often think about other children and how their childhood must be. Ours was a childhood lived in constant fear.

Through my primary-school years, my sleep pattern changed. I become more restless, more nervous. Well, that's what people put it down to. I started telling lies to the teachers about why I was so tired. I was always tired at school, and the teachers could find no explanation why.

Our parents had friends who knew of the violence. One friend had offered Mum a way to escape, but she continued to stay because, in those days, you were told you had to stay married. My mum being Catholic, well, they did not believe in divorce. At this time, Mum was still very devoted to the church.

The beatings were getting more frequent. Our father seemed to explode more often. We finally got the money to move, and we moved to a horse property in another area. It was a bigger house, but there were only two bedrooms inside. I didn't mind, because it meant my brother and I were still together, and I could still protect him well.

In my little mind, that's when I thought our father began to drink more, and constantly. Maybe it was his way of dealing with guilt. The bashings at this house were more public, as we now lived amongst people we knew. The racing fraternity was like a big extended family. Everyone knew what was going on, yet nobody stepped forward to offer any help.

The violence was getting to a point where Mum couldn't even ask him where he was going without him getting agitated. Again, I think that guilt was playing a hand. James and I would often be in our room sitting together holding on for dear life, as he was still too young to understand and I was too young to do anything. But I tried. I would be strong, be the protector of James, always believing and hoping that one day God would answer our prayers.

Our door was often closed to muffle the noise, but we could still hear the punches as he hit her, throwing her into the walls. She would be crying in pain. We would sit there bewildered, not sure whether to go out or sit there until it was over. Always the big unknown in our young minds was whether he would kill her.

Again, the hair was his control. I just cannot imagine the need to do this to another person. Most of the time, we would come out from our room, as listening to our mother being beaten was too much to bear. You have to remember, we were still very young, so we honestly thought this went on in other households. But then there comes the moment where you just know that this only goes on in your house. That in itself is a sadness that only some people ever really feel.

The impact of his aggression was terrifying. It was getting to the point where he would be hitting us too, as we would be trying in desperation to stop this. I still to this day cannot fathom why he beat any of us. I'm also not really sure how Mum found the courage to face people, although no one ever said anything; either they were too scared, or people just didn't want to get involved. She must have been braver than I can imagine, or the shame would have been too much to bear.

Sometimes we'd just wait until it was quiet. It seemed to take forever. Often we would hear the car start up and him drive away, so we knew we were safe—well, safe enough to go and see if Mum was alive. She would be laying there with her shattered body covered in blood, sobbing. As we would go to her, we would have faces so terrified and just so glad she wasn't dead. The blood did not seem to worry us. We just wanted our mum to be okay.

I can't even imagine what she was thinking. She would always try to reassure us and tell me "It will be okay, just look after James." She would stand slowly, steadying her broken body by holding on to something.

I never understood why she stayed. I always thought that if this is what happens, there is no way I'm ever going to get married. I became so cynical for a little girl. *No man will ever do this to me*, I would think.

Mum tried to find the right words to say to two terrified kids, but there really weren't any. Not in our language. I think the silence said it all. She would make her way to the bathroom to clean up, often telling me to take James and go to bed. We would lay there waiting. Eventually she would come in and join me and James in bed. It was just so comforting to have Mum near us. All mums have their spot.

Our mum was so special to us when she had survived another battering. We would all work together to push our wardrobe across the door. This was our way to feel safe so we could get some sleep. Just having Mum in the room with us was sometimes enough. As she would lay there, I would hear her heart breaking. What could she do? There wasn't anyone to help. We were all alone in this cycle of abuse, with nothing to do but pray. At least when Mum was locked in our room, we knew that we would all wake up together, and she would be alive tomorrow.

That was just the best feeling in the world, you know, when you lay with your mum. Mums all have their own smell, and you just feel so safe, and you sometimes don't want the morning to come. We loved our mum so much.

James and I began to tell more and more lies to try to cover up what was happening at home. Lies became easier to tell than the truth. Our sad story seemed to have no ending. Our families never spoke of it—or maybe they just did not recognize it or simply ignored the signs. I'm still uncertain which one it was.

Time was marching by. We were still very young. We lived in a nice house and seemed to have everything we needed, but looks can be deceiving. Behind our closed door was a hell beyond words. Our sleeping had now become a major problem; our bodies rested, but our minds did not. It was like living in a glass bubble, just waiting for it to shatter at any given moment. Raised voices, glass shattering … on and on it went.

We would freeze up inside. It was like your stomach was put through a ringer. The tightness was unbearable, and our little bodies shook as we wondered what terror we would be faced with this night. What would he be subjecting us to? Would she survive another beating? Would she be alive in the morning? These were the thoughts we went through every night. There were no happy thoughts, as there did not seem to be much happiness in our lives.

James and I needed no words. Just a look was all it took, and we both knew the constant punching, kicking, and shoving her into a wall had started again. We would scream and scream, but still it went on.

The beatings continued, the same bullshit. He would beat her into a pulp, we would scream, he would finish the flogging and take himself off to wherever, and she would pick up her shattered body with blood everywhere and, with a broken voice and a broken heart, look at our traumatized faces and lie again. I would take James into our room and wait for her. This was our life.

The same thing would go on week after week. I know I have repeated this, but I want you to understand, this was our life. Domestic violence was an unspoken problem for many women who were and still are subjected to terrible assaults.

As I got older, she taught me to ring the police. They would eventually come, but they were not able to do anything. It was like the husband had this right to beat his wife. The police were useless. I sometimes wonder why I even rang them, but there was always hope of someone maybe wanting to help us.

A hatred for this man was starting to grow in us. We would dread his presence and loath his company, but kids are forgiving. He was still our dad, and there were times when I did love him a great deal. A promise that he would not to do this anymore would fill us with hope, but it would only last as long as his next outburst.

Mum had now become a little wiser. As soon as he started, if she could, she would make a run for it, leaving us behind. It must have been the hardest thing she ever had to do, but self-preservation comes first. James and I would hide while he screamed and she ran up the street for help.

He would turn on us then, often beating us with a horsewhip. I would try to lay over James to protect him, but the pain of the whip would become unbearable. He was smart, only hitting our bodies where marks could be well hidden. He would pick us up in a rage, slapping our faces, demanding that we tell him where she had run off to. The fear was overwhelming. We had to develop an emotional block to this man in order to find some protection from the abuse.

Mum would sometimes be able to get help either from the police or a neighbour, but many people resisted getting involved, and they would turn away. I feel shame for those people. They were cowards. How anybody can turn away from the cries of a beaten woman is so far from anything I can imagine that I cannot comprehend it.

I now wanted to start staying at other family members' houses just to escape the horror, but unbeknownst to James and me, another horror awaited us: child sexual abuse. But that's for another chapter. Just trying to survive at home on his terms was getting more and more difficult. We both developed a great storytelling ability. Lies were with us every day, and by God, we needed them. They made us fit into a world where we didn't belong. Mum also now had become a liar to protect herself. Sometimes I think the shame was just too much.

I recall a night when he arrived home from wherever he had been (it was only later that it was revealed that our father had many affairs). This one night we heard him come in, and we lay there waiting for the explosion. It was always the same thing. He started ranting on and on. Breaking of glass was always a sure sign of what was coming. We would be up and out of our beds in a flash.

She ran this night, and as she ran, he chased her, hurling a small go-kart of James's at her. I don't know if it got her; she just kept running. This was a lucky night, as Mum was able to escape. Even though she had to leave us behind, Mum was busy protecting herself. Self-preservation—it's funny as I write that word again.

I didn't deliberately take on the role of second mother, it just came naturally. It was as though it was given to me, as there was no one else. Mum was trying so hard to protect herself. As I write this book, so many things are becoming clear to me. I'm just starting to understand the long-term impact domestic violence had on James and me.

We moved again. It seemed we did that often. With every move and every new beginning, he would promise the world, promise that there would be no more violence. As kids, we really wanted to believe our dad, but this would only last as long as it took for him to go out again. Maybe a couple of days if we were lucky. The assaults continued with every move.

As small kids, we continued with our nightly prayers. Mum was still quite religious. On bended knees, we would ask God to keep us safe from harm and please, God, keep Mummy safe. Over and over again we'd ask this. I remember asking Mum, "Do you think God might ever hear my prayer? I've been praying for a very long time."

She would just smile and say, "God's a bit busy." This excuse started to wear thin.

There was another move—we had become very nomadic. Our father had started to run an illegal gambling business from home. He had started the game in the bush where people would go, but now it was getting bigger, and more important people were coming, so he improved the standards. Not only was the game illegal to run, but he was as crooked as they come.

We had each other on the weekends. They had become quite tolerable. The weekdays, however, would be hell. He would often be out all night, if we were lucky. He would come home in the morning just as I was getting ready for school. Those were good nights; we got to sleep finally.

After our father's assaults, he would buy Mum flowers, always writing notes of apology with every attack. It was quite bizarre; there was no sense in it. Even today I still don't understand why.

James and I would often watch *Neighbourhood Police*. It was a police series on TV. James used to want to ring them, as they always came when there was trouble. As small children, TV was very real to us. We did not know that life wasn't like TV—not the cruel reality we faced.

Our local police didn't live that far from us, but they did nothing. We would often show up at the police station, two small hysterical children with their mum covered in blood, but always we got the same answer: "We can't do nothing."

The marks he was leaving on her were more evident now. As I got older, I realized that the police were powerless, as it seemed it was a man's right to beat his wife and children. Thank goodness the law has changed, but it is still up to the officer's discretion on whether anybody is charged.

Mum had now stopped trying to hide the marks on her body. She was at the point where she hoped other people would see them. I suppose she was hoping that someone would help her. In the end, it made no difference. Watching her go through this would have a far-reaching impact on James and me.

Our parents would often buy houses that they could renovate. Our father was still running his illegal game. We had moved to another house, but this time our father had started to run his game from a small suburb on the coast. His interest in training horses was minimal, with the game being the main focus.

He came home drunk as usual. We were in bed but heard him pull up. We heard them start arguing. Mum was asking him about an affair she believed he was having. The beating started almost immediately, with him punching her so hard she fell against the wall near my bedroom. By then, James and I were up.

We had seen a lot in our young lives, but nothing could have prepared us for what was to come. Mum grabbed at the wall where there was a large decorative wooden spoon and fork. She grabbed the spoon down and struck him with it. This was the first time I can remember her ever fighting back. It only seemed to make him angrier that Mum had finally found some strength.

He ran out the back. We didn't really know what he was up to. We were just glad Mum was okay. The next minute, through the back door he came like a character out of some horror movie. In disbelief, we realized that he had his chainsaw. Pulling the cord, he turned it on. The noise itself was as terrifying as any I had ever heard.

He kept revving it, *ruumm, ruumm*. James was hysterical, screaming to Mum. To our horror, he kept running at her, putting the chainsaw close to her throat, screaming at her. I can't even remember what he was saying; it was just a blur. Our eyes were like saucers as we stood there still as statues. We did not move—fear had paralysed us.

He just kept it up, running at her, revving the thing. All the while, we just did not move. We did not know what to do. I can't ever remember being that frightened. As he turned around to face James and me, he revved it up again. It seemed to go on forever, but in reality it was only a few minutes. He proceeded to cut down the wall in our dining room. With every cut he made, he would again run at Mum. I have never been so scared or seen anyone else so scared.

Mum was covered in blood from the beating. There was blood everywhere. We saw an opportunity, so we ran over to Mum. This made him even angrier, so he was now running at all of us with this monster in his hands. Every time he ran at us, she would shield us. We were totally hysterical. It was madness now that he had crossed over into. Mum was totally in fear for herself and us. Every time she tried to move, he would run at her with that thing.

It was about midnight, I guess, I'm not really sure—I did not bother to think about the time—when Mum, struggling to stay on her feet, leaned down to James and said, "You have to be brave now. You and your sister have to try to get help."

When he saw Mum whispering to us, he had another swing, revving this thing in our faces. We couldn't move; we were trapped in the corner with Mum. The moment seemed to last for such a long time. Our minds were scrambled. I still to this day cannot recall the whole night. Mum kept screaming at us to go and get help. We were in a sort of daze and just too scared to move.

I was trying to focus on where I could get help. The phone was not an option, as I would have to go past him, and there was no way I was doing that. Thoughts were racing round and round. *Think*, I was saying to myself. *God help us*, I thought. *Well, really anybody will do.* It was the early hours of the morning. The streets would be in darkness, but that was the least scary thing at this moment. All we could think of was that he would cut her head off whilst we were gone.

Paralysed and trapped against the wall, she begged me again to go and get help. Through my broken voice and tears, I said, "What if he kills you before we get back?"

She said again, "You have to be brave. You have to be strong. Now go and take James, go and find anybody."

Whilst he was busy cutting down our wall, I seized the moment and ran out the back door, pulling James. I ran down the street dragging him, as he was still hysterical. We did not want to leave Mum, but there was no other choice. All the while, Mum was hoping he would hit an electrical wire whilst he was cutting the wall down. As he put the chainsaw into the wall, revving it up, he would tell her he was going to cut her fucking head off and cut her up into pieces.

As we ran down the street, I remembered that there was a blacksmith who lived a few houses from us. So that's where we headed. Mum had whispered that to me when we were trapped in the corner with her, but I only just remembered what she said. I think we were too traumatized and our minds were too scrambled to remember what Mum had said to us: that they should be home, probably asleep.

The last thing we'd seen as we left the house was him pinning her back into the corner, running at her, putting the chainsaw up to her throat. This was what we saw as we ran down the road for help in the middle of the night. We visualized that her head would be cut off by the time we got back. The fear made my body shake. My jaw was trembling so much I couldn't speak.

We made our way down the road, terrified of what we might find when we got back home. Our hearts were pounding and tears were choking us as we got to the blacksmith's house and banged on the door, screaming for someone to "Open the door, please help, please open the door."

Finally, with all the commotion, lights came on and the door was opened. The man just stood there for a moment looking at me and James, trying to make sense of our terrified babbling. When our plea for help became clear to him, he went back inside.

It seemed to take forever for him to come back out. James grabbed at me, saying, "He's not going to help, what will we do? We have to go back. Mum might be dead."

I heard the man tell his wife to ring the police. I heard her ask why, and he said, "I don't have time to go into it. Just ring them. It's urgent—a matter of life and death." He emerged from his house holding a rifle.

We followed him back to our house with our hearts low, just not knowing what to expect. Was our mum alive? Was she dead?

When we reached our house, we walked around the back, listening to see if there was any sign of life, a noise, just to know Mum was okay. As we reached the back door, the blacksmith stepped in front of us to protect us from whatever was there. Inside, the wall had fallen completely over onto the floor. The house was a total disaster. We had never seen anything like it before.

Our father had Mum pinned to the corner, and he was putting the chainsaw up to her throat to cut her head off. He was like the devil. Who was this terrible man yelling at our mum, saying, "You are going to die"? We stood there screaming hysterically as he revved it one more time before taking the fatal swing.

Suddenly, the saw shut down. It was like an angel had finally stepped in. The man yelled at our father to step away as he pointed the rifle at him. Our father turned around, still with chainsaw in his hand. Mum now had fallen to her knees. It was a moment of instant relief that she was not going to die, not this time. In total shock, James and I ran to her, grabbing on to her. Mum hugged us and never let go. Well, she did, but not for a little bit. We were so glad she was alive.

The man again told our father to back away or he'd pull the trigger. Finally our father put the chainsaw down, threw his hands up in the air, and mumbled something. Then he took himself off to bed, closing the door behind him. It was surreal.

Shaking and traumatized, we cuddled Mum again. It didn't seem to matter about all the blood as we stood there sobbing. The man asked Mum if there was anything that he could do. Her voice clearly shaken and hoarse from all the yelling, she lifted her battered body and just said, "No, it's okay, he has gone to bed."

The man seemed bewildered and shaken himself. One could only imagine what thoughts must have been running through his head. He leaned down and spoke to James and me, telling us it was going to be okay now. We were still sobbing. He stayed for a few more minutes whilst Mum tried to clean herself up. Her clothes were covered in blood, and her face was again smashed.

The man reluctantly left. The house looked like a bomb had gone off in it, but we did not care. Our mum was alive, and that's all that mattered. Mum told me to take James into his room, as the wall into my room had been cut out. James's room was at the back of the house. We didn't want to leave Mum at all. We were so scared that he was going to wake up again. The chainsaw marks were even in the back of my wardrobe, cut right through.

As James and I waited, she finally hobbled in, pushing James's wardrobe across the doorway. James and I were trying to help as much as we could. We finally lay down to sleep. She sat on the floor reassuring us that it was over for the night and we should go to sleep.

I sometimes wonder what she must have being thinking whilst she sat on that floor waiting for daylight to arrive. Was she asking, "What have I done to deserve this?" All the whys just never got answered. Sitting there in the darkness, Mum must have been exhausted, trying to make sense of what had just happened.

In the morning, we heard him up yelling at her and us to come out and clean up. We woke up trembling, asking her not to go out. We were begging her. We didn't think we could take anymore. Still tired from little sleep and just emotionally drained, Mum pushed the wardrobe to one side and opened the door. He was standing in the kitchen. He had no shame, no remorse. Looking at Mum's battered body, he did not show any reaction at all. I stood there for a moment and wondered, just wondered

The house was a mess, but she refused to clean it up. "You did this," she said, "you clean it up." She pushed James and me towards the back door. We hadn't had anything to eat, and as we made our way outside another argument started. He was abusing her and calling her terrible names, but Mum somehow found a bit of courage. Maybe it was the sitting waiting in the dark, the searching of her soul, that made her say no to him. He had people coming over for lunch. So guess what? He had to clean up the mess all by himself. There was no way in hell James or I would help him.

James and I were just so proud of Mum. it did not matter that her face and body were battered, it was the fact that Mum had seemed strong. Maybe Mum was getting stronger, or maybe the chainsaw attack was nearly her breaking point.

We were outside with Mum. Our dog had had puppies, so we were trying to get them from under the house. The old lady from next door came over to see us. She was making small talk, but Mum was not looking at her. Mum was still covered in blood, as she had not had time to even change.

The woman said to Mum, "Did you hear that maniac last night revving his motorbike outside our houses?"

Mum just smiled and said no, we did not hear anything, but I'm sure the old lady had seen the marks on Mum's face and maybe just worked out for herself that it wasn't really a motorbike. Maybe she did not want to embarrass Mum any more than she was already. I can't even imagine the shame she must have felt. Another lie to tell. It had become part of who we were. People always seemed to want to believe a lie instead of the truth anyway.

The beatings continued. We moved again. Mum was just about at her wits' end. She was as thin as a rake. Her nerves were shattered. The priest used to come to visit her to see how she was. With her health starting to fail, things were getting worse. I used to think, *Is this ever going to end?* Going to school was a nightmare, as we would have to leave her there alone.

James was going to a primary school across the road, so he would go home all the time. He would often meet me at the front gate crying, telling me that she was covered in blood again or was lying on the floor, and our father had beaten her again.

Eventually, she snapped. I'm not really sure what the breaking point was, but it had come. I didn't care why; we just wanted him gone.

Mum went to her priest and told him she could not take anymore. As a Catholic priest, it was his job to encourage her to stay, as divorce was not really the done thing, but even he advised her to leave. The priest told Mum he would write to the Mother Church and explain that if she didn't leave, he would eventually be burying her.

She finally found the courage and told our father to go, but one should never fail to expect the unexpected. He did not go easily. He gave her another thrashing just to remind her what she was going to miss. I'm sure that's what he was thinking.

But he decided he wasn't ready to leave, so he came up with a plan, something to blackmail her with. He kidnapped James and told her that unless she took him back, she would never see James again. He won that time, and the beatings continued. James was so terrified of this man. Myself, I just hated him. I wished he would die every day.

Mum received a phone call one day just out of the blue from the airlines to confirm the booking for an interstate trip. This is what he had told her, that they would go away and start again, but the airline booking was for two adults and a few kids more than just me and James.

Mum sat down and thought about the phone call. She had suspected our father of having an affair with one of her friends for quite some time. She now confronted him with the evidence. This time, the beating nearly killed her. He was pounding her body, kicking her constantly about her face and body. He was saying the most horrific things to her.

Finally he did leave, but the damage was now so bad and had been going on for so long that Mum had a small breakdown. Her frail body was lying on her bed, too weak to move. Mum just had nothing left, no faith, no hope. She had lost all self-respect and self-esteem. All sense of what was right was gone or had been beaten out of her.

She couldn't get out of bed. Mum told me to ring our nana. I asked Nana to come over, as Mum couldn't come to the phone. Nana finally came to help. For James and I, this was the first time our family had realized the extent of the terror we had been put through. My grandparents were horrified and so angry and upset. Realizing that Mum had had a breakdown, Nana rang for the priest. He came over again to counsel Mum. He told her again to divorce our father. He told Mum he'd written to the Pope for permission.

As Mum started to slowly recover, she decided to do some wallpapering to our house like a bit of therapy. Mum still didn't go out much. She was only just beginning to feel like we could make it. Our father had moved out, and for the first time in our lives there was peace and a sense of order. No more bashings, we thought.

Our father went and worked in a roadhouse for a couple of months, and it was like heaven. But it didn't last long. He was back this time angrier and more violent. I remember one particular night, he had come around the house with one of his cronies, a young man nicknamed Slimmy. They forced their way in, smashing the wire door down as James and I screamed.

He pushed past us in a fit of rage, wielding a baseball bat. As he started to swing the bat at Mum, his mate was yelling, "Yeah, go on!" Our father hit, and Slimmy goaded him on. "Hit her, hit her, mate, hit her, smash her, mate."

Mum was screaming hysterically. She yelled at me to go over the road to get our neighbour. As I went to go, Slimmy grabbed me by the arm. I wriggled and punched at him, and he finally let me go. I flew across the road like I had wings. Knocking on the neighbour's door, I tried to explain what was going on. I just wanted him to come. I didn't have time to talk. Our father could have killed Mum by now.

Running back over the road, our neighbour pushed past the young man who was blocking the door so Mum couldn't escape. Slimmy was cheering our father on. Our neighbour grabbed the bat from our father and pushed him into the wall. Thank God he was a big man who did not take shit.

Freeing Mum from the corner, he told her to go over to his house and get his wife to ring the police. By the time the police arrived, our neighbour had pushed our father to the ground and lifted the bat up, saying to him, "Go on, give me a reason." The wimp just sat on the ground. Mum was again covered in blood and shaking—a sight that was oh so familiar to us.

The police went over to our house with Mum. As she walked in, she smacked Slimmy clean across the face. This was the first time I had seen my mum show she still had some fight left in her.

The police took our father with them. They threw him into the paddy wagon, and his limp-dicked friend got taken away as well. There were never any charges, though. The domestic violence laws were still designed not to help women and children.

As Mum was recovering from this attack, our father was planning another one. Only a couple of days later, he rang to ask her if she could meet him out front just to talk. A friend of hers was there helping her, and we begged her not to go. I pleaded with her, but she said, "It's only out in front of the house." We begged her again—it was pathetic that we were begging her not to go. Had she not had enough? But she didn't listen.

He pulled up across the road near the school that James attended. James and I flew up to my room. My window looked out that side. We watched as she walked over there. We were watching like hawks as he opened the back door, where she sat with her legs out of the door.

It was only a couple of minutes later that we heard his car screech and take off. Mum tried to jump out, but her foot got caught in the seatbelt. All we could hear was her screaming as she was dragged down the street. We screamed and ran out the front only to see his car disappear over the hill. We were hysterical.

Mum's friend ran back inside to ring the police. Meanwhile, he had stopped his car just over the hill. It must have knocked Mum out, because when she came to, he was standing over her with an axe. As she struggled to get her foot free, he yelled at her that this was it, he was going to kill her. As he started to swing the axe, she freed her foot. She scrambled along the ground with her heart pounding, and with absolute dread she managed to get to her feet.

She saw a light on in a house across the road. As she made her way to the house, he was right behind her. She got to the front door, pulled open the wire door, and started banging for someone to open the door. He was now on top of her. She fell to the ground kicking on the door, screaming, "Please, someone, open the door!" She kicked harder and yelled louder, with our father now lifting the axe for the fatal blow. Mum thought this was it as she cowered with her hands over her face.

And then the door finally opened, and a man stood there holding a rifle. As he clicked back the gun, Mum fell into his legs, grasping at his legs, holding on. He told our father to put down the axe. Our father stood there with the axe raised high above his head, ready to split her in two.

The man, now shoving the gun into our father's face, said, "Put it down or I will blow your fuckin' head off."

Our father replied, "She is my wife."

The man said, "I don't care. Put it down or I'll pull the trigger."

Mum was shaking with fear. Her heart seemed to stop, and she took a deep breath. The man told her to go inside the house, and he told our father to move away. Our father finally retreated, and the man still stood there pointing the gun at him.

Meanwhile, James and I were beside ourselves not knowing where she was or even if she was still alive. As we waited for the police to come, the phone rang. It was Mum, ringing to let us know she was okay. She told us where she was. James and I ran out of the house and down the street. We ran with our hearts pounding, tears washing our faces, straight past the man who was now standing out in front, still with the gun in his hand. Mum had also rung the police and told them where she was.

She was sitting on the lounge when we ran in. James went to Mum and clung on like a vice, his heart breaking as we looked at Mum's injuries. Her face was covered in blood, with skin also removed from her face where she had been dragged down the road. Her dressing gown—a pink one, I remember—was covered in blood. She couldn't speak; her voice was shaky and her heart was torn apart as she watched the anguish and terror cross our faces. I remember just staring into space.

The unbelievable part is that it was true. No amount of denial or hiding in my make-believe world could erase the fact that he had gone this far. Mum had also rang one of her sisters to come and get James and me, and she arranged for our aunt to pick us up from the house. The police finally arrived. They talked to Mum and the man for a while and decided that we needed to go back to the house so Mum could get some clean clothes, as she needed to go to hospital. Her injuries needed to be looked at. We needed stuff for the next day.

As one of the police officers walked with us to the house, the other drove the car back. Mum stopped in her tracks when she saw that our father's car was at the house. Our hearts sank; we did not want Mum to go into the house. The police escorted her to the door. They found our father sitting on the lounge with the axe across his knee. The police walked in first, and the officer asked him to put the axe down.

He replied, "I can't."

The policeman asked him to put it down, and our father replied, "I'm frightened of my wife."

With that, the policeman slapped him across the face and grabbed the axe. He said, "You piece of shit, you're under arrest."

Our father laughed and said, "She can't charge me."

The policeman said, "I know, but I can. Now get up." With that, the policeman grabbed him, turned him around, and handcuffed him. We were out in the front. As our father approached the front door, he said to Mum, "You wait." The policeman pushed him out of the house. It was terrifying.

Mum went off to hospital. We went to our aunt's. But eventually, we were all back in the same house, and the assaults still went on, night after night. I couldn't take it anymore. It was becoming so unbearable.

I started to rebel; my life seem to go out of control. Between this and the sexual abuse I was experiencing, I now had no respect for myself or anyone else. My schoolwork dropped to an unbelievable low. I just never went to school. It was too hard to face anyone, with the horror that was going on at home. My respect for my mum fell also. Why did she put up with this for so long? James's schoolwork also was suffering.

Eventually, we moved to another house, just the three of us. We ended up in a horrible house, but that's all Mum could afford to buy, as now her money had been divided. Mum started to work at a pub as a barmaid. I was a teenager, and James was a young boy. Mum used to have to work nights, and many a night our father would be creeping around the car park, waiting to attack her. He would follow her home and get her as she was getting out of the car. Again, on and on the assaults went.

He disappeared for a little while somewhere over east, and we had a little peace. It was great. Mum met a fellow whilst working at the pub, a man I had little time for—our younger sister's father, a man who would be part our lives for more than ten years.

But then our father came back, and the attacks became quite bizarre. He would pull up with a couple of women and men, always drunk, falling out of a taxi. The yelling would start. We would be inside and hear the commotion, and we would peek out the window. As soon as we saw it was him, I would ring the police. More times than I can remember, he would be kicking in our front door, smashing against the glass to get into the house. You could almost bet the police would be late, and he'd get a chance to do what he come to do—more bashings, more terror.

After so many years of this horror, I remember thinking I couldn't take it anymore. It got to the point where death looked better. It would stop everything. My way of dealing with all of it was to detach myself completely—mentally, physically, anywhere there was no pain. I remember looking up to the sky and saying to God that I would never stay with a man who hit me, and to this day, I haven't.

One time I ran into the kitchen and grabbed a knife. As I ran back in, he had Mum by the hair and was pulling her down so he could knee her in the face. He saw I had a knife and that I wanted to kill him. I wanted him dead. James was in the middle, trying to help free Mum's hair. Our father grabbed me with his free hand as I was swinging the knife at him. I kept yelling, "Why don't you just die?"

The police came, and I put the knife down when the policeman asked me to. The officers told our father to leave again. *I will run away, far away,*

I would say to myself. I would daydream about my world in which there was no bashing, no violence. We would be safe in my world. My mind would say no more, and my subconscious mind would step in and remind me of our reality. Was there ever going to be a reckoning?

We used to spend at least three nights a week in the local motel, or sometimes we would have to sleep in the car. He would ring us now to tell us he was on his way. Some nights he would bluff, but usually he would come. I would start to get things happening whilst Mum was on the phone with him. I would grab clothes for everyone and whatever else was needed. I would have the house ready to be locked up, and me and James would be in the car waiting for her. We would leave. It was just something that we did.

Some nights we would argue about whether to go or stay. A couple of times, when Mum didn't want to come, I would tell her that we would run away. It was as if the urgency in our voices wasn't enough. Sometimes we would return in the morning to find the front door kicked in, and we would sit in the car too terrified to go in, as he still could be there. It was a feeling of absolute dread. My heart would be racing, my body shaking from holding on to the stress. It would sit across my shoulders. It was just terrible. But most times, he would have left the house.

He would always leave a terrible mess. Sometimes we would find knives in the bedrooms or hidden outside in the garden. It was an ugly time in our lives. It just seemed to be out of control.

For a while, the attacks died down. The man our mother was seeing was over quite a lot, so our father's attacks were now random. Another night he came and Mum's boyfriend was there, and a big argument started in the hallway of our house. Our father was beating the living shit out of her whilst her drunken boyfriend stood there watching. I remember ringing the police, and then I went into the kitchen and grabbed a knife.

He had hold of her hair, and he kept kneeing her in the face again—a favourite party trick. James was hysterical. I pulled on him to try to get him to release her, but he just pushed me away. With that, I pulled out the knife and told him I was going to stab him, and this time I wasn't going to miss. As I lunged at him, he let go of Mum, grabbed my arm, and slapped me across the face. As he turned to get Mum again, I jumped on his back and put my arms around his throat, trying to strangle him.

When the police finally ran into the house and grabbed our father, I remember Mum walking over and slapping her boyfriend across the face. This was probably the last serious assault that I can remember.

Our father had also begun forcing himself on her whilst we weren't there. James would come home at lunchtime and find her covered in blood, clothes ripped off her. James would get beside himself with fear, as our father again had tried to abduct him. James become so frightened that he never wanted to leave the house. I had gotten to the point where I just didn't care anymore—why should I care if Mum didn't? That's what was in my head, although it was not true at all.

We moved up the road from Mum's parents. Peace came at such a huge cost. The violence James and I witnessed would be embedded in our minds forever. James used violence in his life, as he believed that it was a controlling factor. He learned to have no respect for woman, as he saw what our mother put up with for years. Embedded in James's mind was that being violent was expected. That's what we grew up with.

Myself, I detested violence. When a man became aggressive with me, I was gone. I would never let a man ever do to me what I saw our father do to our mother.

As I close this chapter, I do realize that some people have lived through more, but why should anyone—adults or children—put up with it? It stays with you forever. Today the laws on domestic violence have come a long way, just not far enough. I'm surprised our mother even lived through the attacks, but somehow she survived.

So many different courses are available for men and woman. Anger management is good. James did this course, as he tried for years to get his anger under control. He had been angry for a long time, and it festered inside until it burst open like a pussy sore.

Don't be a victim. Do more for yourself and do more for your children. The violence we witnessed was pounded into our lives. It wasn't something that we wanted. No one ever asks for this. Beware of the trap that so many people fall for. There is a way out—just find the strength to get out. If you are the aggressor, find the help you need to break the cycle of violence before it breaks you. Do it for yourself first and for your family.

Even now as I counsel children, when they ask me, "Why does my mum stay?" I have no real answer for them. I just tell them that it will end one day. They will grow up and be able to make real choices in their lives. I explain to them that I don't think good men hit women. That's my opinion, but what are these women saying to their children? That it's okay for a man to hit you? Is that what love is about? Are you telling your boys they can hit a woman and she'll stay? Is this the message you want your sons to have?

*Evil is not commited by the perpetrator but also by the people that stand by and do nothing*

# CHAPTER 2

## *Sexual Abuse*

There are moments even today when thinking about this terrible part of my life makes me physically ill. This is truly an emotionally fucked-up ride. Sexual child abuse—the very meaning of these words makes my whole body cringe. I have an overwhelming feeling of disgust and a shame that has gone on in my life for a very long time. There are still so many things that I have no answer for.

I still hesitate to say that I no longer feel like a victim, even after many years of counselling. It's hard to break free of all the guilt that holds you there. It's like a living force that has no solid shape. As much as I have dealt with my child abuse well, I tell anyone who is a survivor that you really only ever deal with what you can, and there are still parts I find hard to deal with. Even now, some of it makes my skin crawl, and I become anxious and agitated.

James had only started to deal with his abuse in the last few years of his life. He just couldn't cope with being a survivor of child abuse. We had only been openly discussing some parts of it before his death.

I believe that I am a survivor. I have been battling these demons for more years than I can remember. I don't blame this alone for certain events in my life, but the impact playing out in our lives is a constant reminder that even more than the violence we were subjected to, this horror changed our lives indelibly and forever. It changed our opinions of ourselves and drained whatever self-esteem or self-respect we had left.

It was a horror that words can never fully describe. You would have to be a survivor yourself to understand. Not that I think for one moment that anyone deserves this to happen to them; it's just that sometimes people don't get the full impact.

This horror was inflicted on us in the midst of the terror at home. Child molesters pick their victims. They groom the child and sometimes the parent. We must have looked like easy targets, as it was impossible to have any peace at home, so going to someone else's place seemed like an escape. Little did we know that what we were escaping to was far worse.

The child abuse was inflicted on us by someone we all trusted, someone we loved. Sending us away sometimes, Mum would think that we would be safe from the horror at home, as our parents were so caught up in their own drama. Our father was living his life totally out of control, and Mum was trying to survive her own demons or her own guilt, I'm not really sure which one; maybe it was both.

As I said, it had only been in the last couple of years of his life that James felt comfortable even talking about this taboo subject. We had a mutual friend who James had only just started to tell things to. She would come to me and ask me things about whatever James had mentioned. It was like he needed to verify certain things in his life that made no sense.

I had been seeing a counsellor for many years as I struggled desperately to come to terms with this part of our lives. James had also been attending therapy for this and other things. Child sexual abuse strips away your very soul, and then when you finally have the courage to face the world with these demons, the world shudders with denial, as this is its protection to cover the guilt. Those who wish to be in denial and dismiss the truth are themselves responsible for the child molesters amongst us.

It is easy to deny the truth, as the truth itself is so painful. Statistics show one in three girls and one in six boys are molested before they are eighteen by someone they trust. My own experience with this subject runs raw to my bones. This was part of the unspoken truth between James and me, something that in my lifetime I will never forget. It's something that I have learned to live with. James never really discussed the extent of the sexual abuse against him. It was something that he wanted to do, something we had planned, but my brother took his secrets to his grave. I can only recall my own experiences in this matter and what I briefly know about what James experienced.

When I was in high school, sex ed, as it's called, didn't get taught to us until year 9. I remember being in class listening to the teacher as what she was saying became blurred to my hearing. She was talking about stranger danger and how it was wrong if people touched us in certain ways that weren't appropriate or made us feel uncomfortable. I began to wiggle in my seat. I felt agitated and very uncomfortable. My head felt heavy and foggy.

I was trying to make sense of what she was saying. My mind was racing, and I guess I had a blank look on my face just trying to comprehend what she was saying. Then *bam*, the bombshell dropped. *Fuck*, I said to myself. I knew all of those things, but until now no one had told me they were wrong. This awful feeling I had inside, it was like an alien was going to jump right out of my stomach. I remember feeling unwell. There was a feeling of utter confusion, a blurred mist.

I pretended to myself that this was not true and I was like everyone else, but I couldn't speak. The other children were talking about it quite openly, and I just wanted to disappear. I kept thinking, *Please don't ask me any questions.* I was desperate for the class to end. Finally the siren rang and we were dismissed. I remember just walking out of school. I couldn't leave fast enough. I needed to think. I needed to understand.

I was very confused, because my uncle was no stranger—he was my family.

Those early days I think must have been the most awful for me. At fourteen, your vision of the world can be easily shattered. The shame I felt I cannot put into words. There was no one I could talk to, and in no way did I want to share this terrible secret. I was going to forget what he had done, push it back so far in my memory I just wouldn't remember it at all. Gone, gone. I didn't want to even think about all those terrible things.

My teenage years were out of control as I tried to silence the terrible voice inside my head. I tried desperately to hide and forget the demons that were inside of my soul, or what was left of it. I felt the very foundation of my soul had been damaged so much that God himself couldn't help me.

In this terrible darkness, there was no light. It's so sad for any young person to feel such emptiness These years whizzed past in a total blur. I would have to grab hold, because my life was spiralling out of control. All the terrible things I did to myself—drinking to forget, being promiscuous, not even remembering sometimes who I had slept with—I did to keep from remembering. Yet the memories would not fade. I could not hide from the truth; it always caught me when I least expected.

I was about twenty-four when the nightmares I was having started getting worse. They were becoming very real and quite frightening. I had pushed things so far down into my subconscious that I didn't think they would ever come back. But that's just it: they sneak in, and you start to question yourself. Memories started to form that I didn't want to know about. It became very distressing, and the shame I felt was indescribable.

This went on for quite some time, with me slowly beginning to understand some parts of my life. My subconscious was preparing me for a journey back to a place that I didn't want to go. A feeling of dread, a sinking feeling that sat in the pit of my gut, was telling me it was time to put my life back together. My mind was trying to unscramble a past that I didn't care for but was forcing its way through.

I would dread going to sleep, as it seemed every time I did the memories came back. I woke from sleep screaming in the middle of the night. Talking in my sleep also became a problem. My mind was going to make me remember even though I didn't want to. I kept thinking, *I don't want to remember, it was too awful.* I kept saying to those memories, *Go away, you are not welcome here, leave!* But Pandora's box was slowing opening. There was nowhere to run, nowhere to hide. You can't hide from yourself.

It was only small things at first. I think that's the mind's way of getting you to deal with it. When the smaller memories became big memories, it was so very scary, and also very confusing. It's like, *Fuck, did I really have those things done to me? Did I let them do that to me? Why didn't I stop it? Why didn't anyone help?* I remember I started to ring helplines. It was like this part of my life opened up, and I didn't want to be there.

My whole life seemed to be falling apart, with no way of stopping it. It was like I was screaming and no one could hear me. I was screaming in my mind. I just didn't want to remember. I become desperate for someone to help, listen, anything. I was drowning with no lifeguard to pull me out.

I would sit for hours trying to digest this mess in my mind. Could so many horrible things have happened to one person? The helplines were great, talking me through some very bad moments. Being out of control helped me in my earlier years, as most people just thought I was wild and unmanageable. My marriage was breaking down; it was like one day I woke up and thought, *Why am I married to this man? I don't love him. He isn't what I dreamed my husband would be.* Was this my way of punishing myself even more? Where could I go from here? As my life was swirling in a direction I didn't want to go, I was pulling in another direction. But it was time—time to face my demons, time to find a way to replenish my soul and to be whole again.

At the very beginning, there were many disbelievers. I'm sure they're still about, but I believe those disbelievers have an agenda all their own. They have their own demons to hide; maybe in their own closets they have their own skeletons that they don't want to come out, because then they would have to face their own truths. Who knows? It made the persecution and lies told about me easier for them.

I do not hate these people for what they did or didn't do. I actually pity them, for I believe their day of reckoning will come. This is when you learn who is the strongest one. I believe that survivors of child abuse are the strongest people I know.

The people who had been talking to me on the helplines advised me to tell my parents, so I rang and asked them both to come with their partners. Interestingly enough, I had started speaking to our father again. Thinking back now, I really don't know why I bothered. Maybe I thought he needed another chance to redeem himself from some of the terrible things he had done, but there you go. I was so wrong. It didn't matter how much I wanted my father to care—he simply did not.

As I prepared for my parents, I kept thinking that our father had a chance now to be the father he never was to James and me. Let's see if he could man up. I believed that my mother most of all would need extra support, as she had never seen it coming. Because of all the violence at home, the child sexual abuse was missed. Such abuse was something that wasn't openly discussed or something that had never happened in our family before. There were no indicators for them to look for, no signs along the way.

Nowadays it is drilled into us all. Children are taught from early childhood. But even with all the teaching, there is still an increase in child sexual abuse. So I ask, what is it we are doing wrong? What aren't we teaching our children? Can more be done to protect the innocent?

Waiting for my parents to come seemed to take forever, but finally I heard cars pull up. They had arrived. As they entered, both of them looked puzzled. They sat down, and I quietly observed them to see if they had any idea, but no.

One of my father's sisters had come along. Maybe she was hiding some demons of her own. Maybe there was something in the past that she was unsure of. Maybe she was there to protect someone. There had been rumours over the years that the man she married had molested her daughter, but this was their shame to hide, not mine. I later found out that she was only there to find out the name of the person who had molested James and me, and to make sure it was not someone close to her home.

As I looked at their faces and cleared my throat, I was feeling very nervous. I said that I had something terrible I had to discuss with them. The pit of my stomach felt like there was concrete in it. I was shaking with nerves. My jaw was shaking, and I was desperately trying to hold my composure. I blurted out the words any parent would hate to hear: "I was sexually abused as a child."

A silence came as they all looked at me. It seemed like forever before anyone spoke. My father was the first to speak, but the tone and sharpness in his voice was as cold as snow. He blurted out, "It wasn't my fault!" before I had even said anything. He just went crazy. I never blamed him, but he was ranting and raving like a madman. He jumped up out his seat and was moving about.

Mum went grey in front of my eyes. Her face said it all. Her mind was racing, sifting through her own memories. She held her head in her hands, her mind whirring, trying to remember anything. What had she done? What had she sent us into? Her mind kept trying desperately to remember.

I suddenly stopped and thought, *They can't handle this*. Mum thought she was protecting us by sending us there, away from the constant abuse at home. How could this have happened? Mum said she blamed our father. He was still ranting. They really did not know about this at all. They had no idea of the nightmare we were subjected to, even more than what was going on at home. It was clear they were both at a loss.

I felt a great sadness for Mum; she thought we would be safe there. My father could not really disappoint me anymore, as he had disappointed me my whole life. He sat there taking no blame, thinking, *We will just call her a liar, and then I won't have to believe and I won't have to take any responsibility for making my children go there.* The truth was just too much for him to deal with.

I didn't blame either one of my parents for what happened. They did not commit these offences against us; an evil man did. Mum realized the part she played in this, and her guilt will last forever. Our father felt no guilt, as to feel anything at all you have to be human first, a quality he lacks.

James did blame our parents. He believed that if our father hadn't done the things he did at home, we wouldn't have been made to go there. Mum he blamed for staying, because if she hadn't, again we would have been saved from those events.

Realizing for the first time that maybe your children's bad behaviours were more than just responding to the domestic violence is pretty shattering for anyone—especially for parents, as they have to live with the guilt. It's probably only now that we understand our behaviour patterns and why we were sometimes uncontrollable. James would often refuse to go to our uncle's house. He would throw the biggest tantrum and literally turn blue from holding his breath. It was only when forced to go with the promise of returning home later that he would agree. It was always done under duress.

I would sit and hold my breath as my body stiffened. My body became so stressed. I cringed to think of what James must have witnessed. I feel a disgust in myself and a feeling of total hopelessness that at times I could have easily gone in another direction. It is hard not blame myself as I sit here thinking about what to write and how to write it so it will be acceptable for people to read. What will I feel comfortable revealing?

My earliest memories of these horrible events are from when I was a young girl. I used to be sent to our auntie and uncle's place on weekends, as Mum and Dad would be running the game. James came a few times, not as often as I did. It was a Saturday night. I was sitting there with my auntie and uncle. She got up to put one of the kids down; they had two children younger than me. Their house was at peace. I never witnessed any violence. There were no beatings. It seemed like heaven to me.

After she put the kids down this particular night, my auntie went to have a shower. When she stepped into the bathroom, I was left alone with my uncle. We were watching TV and just chatting as usual. He was sitting next to me. I was feeling totally safe, and then suddenly without any warning he grabbed my hand and put it down the front of his pants. He made me grab hold of something that I had never felt (which, as I got older, I understood was his penis). He forced me to hold it.

The more I struggled for him to release my hand, the harder he held on. Not really understanding what it was that I was doing, I began to get scared. This seem to go on forever, but realistically, it was only as long as my auntie was in the shower. Finally I heard the bathroom door open, and with that he released my hand. I quickly moved away. She came out of the bathroom and told me to get ready for bed.

I went straight up to my room, and I remember thinking, *Oh gosh, that was horrible. Gosh, I hope he doesn't do that again.* I felt very confused and, for the first time in that house, very frightened. I used to sleep in their eldest child's room. As I lay there, my auntie came to tuck me in. I was so glad it was her, as my uncle had scared me, and I did not know how to feel. I used to think she was great. She was younger than Mum, and I thought she was pretty cool. She leaned over and gave me a kiss and said, "Sweet dreams. We will have fun tomorrow." She was the best.

And then, without any warning, my uncle came in. I just froze. I didn't want to do what he had just made me do in the lounge room. It was disgusting, that hard thing he made me hold. To my horror, he pulled back the covers and began to molest me again. I was stiff with fear. He leaned over and told me this was our secret game and that no one else could know. He began doing things to me that made me feel very uncomfortable. It was all too horrible. I just did not know what to do.

Suddenly my auntie called him. He removed his hand and smiled at me as he left the room. I lay there for a while trying to work out what he had done. No explanation came to mind. I was very young and didn't understand any of it, so I drifted off to sleep.

Finally morning come, and the kids were awake. This was the best time. I loved my cousins. We used to have so much fun. My auntie was in the kitchen, and my uncle was laying in bed. He would call us all in and begin to play around, tickling us, throwing us, and giving us horsey rides.

What I realize now is that he was grooming me. As he was playing these games, his hand would always slip and touch me inappropriately. He used to make a joke of it so I didn't really think anything was wrong. But my little mind had a new memory in it, of him touching me in bed and making me touch him. I remember thinking, *He must do this to all of us, so if no one else says it's wrong, then maybe it isn't.* I enjoyed the fact that he actually paid attention to me. But deep inside, my tummy was tight.

I remember thinking about what had happened on the way home. They would often drive us home the next day. As we approached our house, my heart would sink into the back of my chest. Going home meant going home to the horror of abuse. What had happened at my uncle's home felt very different for me. I didn't really have any idea what had happened. I figured this must be the way things are. I honestly thought what was happening in my own home went on everywhere, so why would this be any different?

The next visit to my auntie and uncle's house came around pretty quick. James was staying over this time, so that was great. But it seemed every time my uncle got a chance, he was now grabbing me or cuddling me, more than he usually did. At first, I didn't mind, as I received no affection from my own father.

My uncle had a big shed in his backyard. He would always try to get us down there. James would go with him, as I was too busy playing with the children. I remember being in the shed a few times, and all he wanted to do was show us porn magazines. Well, I didn't know that's what they were until later on in life. All I knew at the time was that they were filled with people with no clothes on, something we used to laugh at.

James would coming running out of the shed most times. I never really knew what went on in there, but it was getting to the point that James rarely left my side whilst we were at that house. He hated being alone with our uncle.

The molestation was now on a roll. Every time I stayed, my uncle would be at me. He was touching me more and more. He began to hurt me. He was now doing things to my little body that caused great pain. I remember telling him that it hurt, and he would say and do the most bizarre thing to me. He would say, "I'm sorry, let me kiss it better," and so another improper act was taught to me. It had no name, as it had never been done to me before. I remember not really understanding what he was doing, but this didn't hurt at all. Not as much as the other thing he was doing to me, anyway.

My small body was feeling strange. I had never felt this before. How does a young girl understand her body? The feeling of enjoyment was not for a little girl's body, but it happens because our bodies don't understand. I used to think, *My parents don't do this*, and I would ask him. He would say that I was special, and this was our secret. I was his special girl. I felt like he really loved me. So I would shrug my shoulders and think, *Well, he is older than me, so it must be right.*

This went on all the time. I lacked the knowledge and understanding that what was going on was wrong. James was now refusing to stay there at all. I would go on my own, and most times my uncle would get me in bed.

He was now hurting me more and more. His hand would be doing things that I simply did not like, but because he was so much bigger than me, I could not do anything to get him to stop. His other hand would be forcing my hand down his pants and making me grab hold of that horrible thing. I remember that sometimes this stuff would come out. It was warm and wet and felt horrible to me. He was always prepared with a towel or something to wipe it up with.

I didn't really like this game, as he called it. It made me feel very uncomfortable, but I think these were the small things that he was doing to me. I guess he was priming me up to the big event.

We would often go to the drive-in. This was a family thing. He would always make sure that I sat behind him so he could put his hand around the back and touch me. It was going on all the time. He was just at me.

Finally, for James to come, it was agreed that he would drive us home later. I have a clear memory of the first time he drove us home on drive-in night. We were nearly home. I was in the front and James was asleep in the back. Well, I'm sure that's what our uncle thought, anyway.

He pulled the car over to the side and got out. I asked him why we were stopping, but he never answered me. He came around to my door, opened it up, and grabbed me. He turned me around to face him and took my PJs off from the waist down. He began to do the same thing to me as usual; I would just lay there, not really knowing what to do. Sometimes he would masturbate over my body and then clean it up. He would lie on me sometimes and rub his body on mine. Finally it was over, and home we would go. Home to hell, as I would think of it.

This continued on and on. It had now become routine for me, although I was beginning to feel more and more uncomfortable with what he was doing. I mastered escaping into another world, my world, where all things were good and there was no violence and surely none of *this*. My world was my escape, and this allowed me to just dismiss what was happening to me all the time. My world was full of good dads who did not hurt their families and good people who did not hurt their special girls.

I would often assume that James was asleep, but it wasn't until later years that James told me that most of the time he was awake. I felt so sick and dirty. To think he was awake! He would never have understood what was going on. Hell, *I* didn't. But I cannot describe the terrible, terrible shame I felt.

Our minds were getting more and more fucked up with every beating, every sexual attack. I used to think that life was pretty fucked. As I start to recall different events in my life, I feel a tension in my body that I haven't felt for a long time, an uneasy feeling of guilt and shame all in one.

I remember during these terrible times in my life my heart would be full of dread. My young body was reacting in ways that I didn't understand. My childhood was robbed from me in more ways than one. I'm not really sure which was worse as I try to digest everything that happened to me. The abuse by this man who was trusted by our parents went on and on.

At this point, I will go back to when I told my parents. It was decided between all of us that James would not be told yet, as he was very volatile and oozed aggression. Not for one moment did I not think my uncle deserved to be thrashed to within a inch of his life; I just wanted to do something right. We didn't think James could handle the truth, so at this point he wasn't told.

Mum went away for a weekend, and it was then that James started ringing me, continuously quizzing me about what was wrong. It's interesting to note that while James and I had never discussed these things with each other, he knew somehow that I was struggling. He was concerned that my life was falling apart with no explanation. I kept going around in circles, trying to avoid the subject. He would not stop questioning; it was like he was reading my thoughts straight out of my mind. He knew, all right.

He kept ringing me to ask what was wrong, and he kept on asking me why my life was in such a mess again. He asked what had caused it. I would say, "It's like my whole world is not how I knew it." I told him that I was lost, and I was trying to find my way back. But my reality was so terrible. I wondered if the journey forward was worth all the pain. Somehow I had talked myself into going into this dark and terrible time and trying to sort it out the best way I could.

James started acting strange, and his voice was shaking as we talked about my struggle. Then he said the man's name. I didn't answer. I didn't need to. The unspoken truth had been spoken. It was like we had a line to each other's memories.

He went insane then, screaming at me over the phone. I rang Mum to come home urgently. James was going crazy. He jumped on his Harley and drove to where they lived. Of course, the gutless prick hid inside the house and sent our auntie out to greet a man so full of anger and rage.

James was very distressed. He was crying, angry, and totally not in control. He pulled out a weapon—a gun—and asked her where he was. She said he was not there. With that, James asked her once, "Did you know it was going on?"

She replied, "Yes, but I didn't know any other way."

James became even more distressed and very angry. For the first time in a long time, he was faced with a situation in which he had no control. He spoke to her for a while. He told me he asked her, while he had the gun pointed at her, did she know how long it had been going on? James told me she was crying and answered him, "A long time, but I did not know how to stop it. I did not know any different." She told James that she had been molested by a close relative.

James put the gun away. He later told me that he could not remember ever being that distressed in his life. His whole world was now being looked at through a shattered child's eyes The child who once was now filled his head with memories. I'm not too sure what else was said between them. James hopped back onto his bike, and he went to a mate's place—a bikie from the Satan's Sons, Mat, who had been his mate for a long time. I can't even imagine what James said to him, but I suppose being James's mate, he just came for support. Interesting that although James was a member of the Devil's Dogs at the time, he went to his Satan's Sons mate.

They drove to our father's house, where I was. Seeing him pull up, I was as fearful as I had ever been. James stormed into the house with his mate. He was totally out of control at this stage. No one could talk to him. He grabbed me and threw me into a wall. He threw me into one of the bedrooms. Our father tried to intervene, but James pushed him away, cracking his ribs in the process.

James closed the door to the bedroom. He grabbed at me and threw me all around the room until finally he broke down. The distress was obvious in his face. He was sobbing and was not coping with the situation. I was not angry at him. I felt a sadness for my brother, as now it was clear his memories were back to haunt him as well. He would not be able to cope.

We just sat there with that silent truth. No words have to be spoken in that moment when truth is all there is. His head fell into his hands as he sobbed. He looked at me and said, "Why now?"

I replied, "It's time now, James. My life has been so fucked up for such a long time."

He replied, "You have opened Pandora's box, and I'm not ready to look in there yet." His heart was breaking. A shattered man was sitting there beside me, a man whose life had been dealt a huge blow. He sat there for a while with me just talking about it. He couldn't get his head around it.

Looking at him, I saw the boy who couldn't protect me or himself. This man in front of me who had made it his life's journey to have no one ever hurt him was crushed. If there was ever a moment in time that I loved my brother most, it was then.

Slowly calming down, he got up and went to wash his face. He was more angry at me for not telling him straight away. He wanted to be with me through this terrible ordeal. He offered support and had this amazing empathy. He had lived what I had lived; his pain was my pain.

He left our father's and went to Mum's. She was angry because he had hurt me. She yelled at him, and he just sat there sobbing, his head in his hands, his heart heavy with pain He was back to where he did not want to be, a place he had chosen to forget, a place where his soul was damaged. Mum described him to me as a little boy lost.

He sat there for a long time trying desperately to get his head around it and trying to sort through his own feelings. Mum had a brother who lived down the road, an uncle who James loved dearly. He was also a favourite of mine. We called him Uncle T-bear. James went down there. I just think he needed some comforting. He was deeply agitated and very confused. I think he needed someone just to be there for him.

He was feeling an overwhelming grief from a childhood full of terrible things. This unspoken part was just too hard for him to take on all at once. This silent truth had been hidden for such a long time. Uncle T-bear just sat with him. James was safe. Uncle T-bear did not have to comment, he just sat there, and that was enough for James.

It did eventually settle down, and I proceeded to have my abusive uncle charged. That was very confrontational. It was a nightmare having to remember small details of what he had done, because you worry, *Did I miss a detail? Did I remember it right? Did I tell them everything?* The people from the sexual assault team were great; they were so helpful. The police were great, too. They were very gentle in their approach.

He was charged with a number of offenses. All the while, the blame game continued. It's funny how people try to shift blame. There was only one person to blame, and that was the child molester.

We eventually were ready for trial. James took another trip down to their house, looking for him. Again, sadly, he hid. Our auntie dealt with James again. Ranting and raving, James screamed at her, "Where is he?" James had his pistol; he just wanted the man to be dead. Our auntie said he wasn't there. Who knows? That's her burden to bear. Mum rang the police officer in charge of my case and explained to him where James was. She was very concerned. He came to our house and waited for James.

The police officer had come alone, which was very unusual. He met James at the gate. James was an emotional wreck. He sat and talked to the policeman for a few hours. James was feeling an overwhelming uselessness that he couldn't describe. The police officer was sympathetic without being critical. He said to James, "Come on, let's go out the back and spar." He was also into kick-boxing. He wasn't trying to provoke James, just trying to get him to think rationally.

The trial came, and it was a disaster. Well, not really—it freed me from the demon that had occupied my soul. Sometimes people protect the guilty in order to hide their own truth. Their own demons could be exposed, so let's crucify her one more time. These people had their own agenda. They protected him in order to hide even more terrible things that had gone on, terrible things that they themselves had turned a blind eye to. Their own past could have been exposed. So it was my head, my heart, my life they fucked up one more time.

I ask James to join me. He said at the time he wasn't ready to do that just yet. He wasn't ready to face that part of his life. He told me, though, that maybe one day he would be ready. Unfortunately, that can't happen now, but before his death he had gotten the transcripts from my trial, and he had also spoken to the police about his own abuse. I will never know now what really happened to him.

Now back to the molestation. After many years of counselling, more and more memories were coming back to me. I was totally distraught and filled with disbelief at what my mind was making me remember—things that even I questioned how someone could do that to me or how could they make me do it. My young world was filled with things that I thought were normal, so this was what must go on.

I remember being at my counsellor's office, and we were just chatting about stuff when suddenly the subject of child abuse came up. I was fidgeting more than normal. A feeling of tension sat in my shoulders and my gut tightened into knots. I described something that he made participate in, something that I found so distressing that the actual words just wouldn't come. Sitting there distraught, tears welled into my eyes as we discussed it. I felt shame and a guilt that is not mine, it is his for the terrible things he did to me. As far as I have come with dealing with my abuse, this is one thing I haven't got past, and I don't really know if that will be possible for me.

My counsellor always tells me it is not my fault. Child molesters do things to children for two reasons: because they want to and because they can. Going home that night, I was feeling a bit strange, like an uneasy kind of feeling. It was just me and the kids there, and a memory of an event was sort of flickering into my mind—not a pleasant memory, a most disturbing one. At first I tried to dismiss it as being too horrible to want to think of, but no amount of busyness could rid me of it this memory. It had been pushed so far back it just came bursting through.

I grabbed the wall to steady myself. I was clearly shaken. The pain that I was feeling was indescribable. What was my body trying to tell me? I sat down on my step. The kids were busy playing, so me just sitting there wasn't a disturbance to them.

I grasped my chest, as my breathing had become shallow. My legs felt heavy. My heart was racing as I began to remember a time when my little body was torn in two.

I was very young. We were on our way home as usual. It was movie night. The same routine applied—we would stop at the same place—but this time was a bit different. He went to his boot for something I couldn't see. I didn't really want to. I just knew what was going to come … or so I thought.

I would usually drift off into my own little world. There, no one got hurt. As I sat there waiting, the door suddenly opened. He had something in his hands. He pulled me out of the car and laid something over the seat, and then he put me back into the car. He pulled my PJ pants off, but strangely he removed my top as well, something I couldn't recall before. I thought, *What is going on?* I was getting a lot more scared than before.

It started the same, with him kissing me. I used to move my head a lot; it was awful. It was like a dog slobbering on your face. Then the act would start. This is where I would just leave my body and be somewhere else. He began to do things again to my little body that just downright hurt. This always was uncomfortable.

Then *pow,* he was lying on top of me. Sometimes he did this and would rub himself up and down on me. But this night was different. I could feel this *thing.* It felt hard. He was forcing my legs further apart and now hurting me more. I started to make more noise, forgetting that James was in the back. I was now crying and getting louder.

He put his hand over my mouth so I couldn't scream. I could not move—my little body was under his weight. My God, the pain was terrifying. My body was being forced open by this thing between my legs. I couldn't scream; no noise would come out. *Please someone hear me,* but his hand was firmly over my mouth. With no voice to be heard and no one to stop this pain, I thought my small body was going to split in half.

After the event, I remember lying there sobbing and staring up at the roof of the car, my heart thumping almost to the point where I thought it was coming out of my skin. My body was wet with his perspiration. The smell I will always remember. He went and dressed himself. He had a wet cloth, and he was begging to clean me. I looked, and there was blood.

I begin to panic, breathing really fast and shallow. I thought I was dying. I began to cry even more. He grabbed me really hard on the arm and told me it was okay. He told me the blood came from him, and he was really sorry for getting it on me. I told him he hurt me. He cuddled me and told me it was okay, but we can't tell anyone.

The pain in my groin was so sharp. I had never felt such terrible pain. The pain was burning and there was still blood coming out of me. *Please God, don't let me die*, I remember thinking. I just did not know how to feel. *He must love me even though he hurt me. He said he was sorry.*

He finally cleaned everything up. James I thought was asleep, but unbeknownst to me, he had witnessed the whole thing. What must he have thought? He was only a young boy. He told me once he was sorry, but at such a young age he didn't know what to do. He thought I was going to die. He told me he could hear my muffled cry, but he was too scared to do anything. What damage was to come from this!

This terrible event changed my life forever. A child's body, a man's world, my innocence robbed in one night. To this day, I carry a sadness, not only for me but for James too, as his life was also changed forever. I think that of all the sexual abuse I received from this man, this one event is what would become embedded in my life.

The pain I obviously learned to deal with, as I have no memory of complaining to anyone. Not that I think they would have believed me. Back then, they were so caught up in their own world that I was just becoming more and more of a problem. My grades were dropping at school. Mum would put it down to the domestic violence, never thinking that anything like this was going on. I just went with the flow, always thinking this was normal, not knowing it was an evil far beyond words.

I'm not sure how many times he actually had sexual intercourse with me. It's something my mind didn't want me to keep track of. The molestation continued for many more years. I remember the first time he put his body part in my mouth. I thought I was going to die. It was the most awful thing I can remember.

He grabbed me, told me to open my mouth, and forced his body part into my mouth. I tried not to choke. I couldn't get it out of my mouth. He held his hand there. I had tears rolling down my face. It was so awful, this hard pulsating thing in my mouth. Then after a while this horrible stuff would be in my mouth. It was warm and tasted disgusting. I had never tasted anything like it before. I would spit as much out as I could, thinking, *Yuck, that's gross.*

I figured there was no one to help me, so this must be right. This was my reality, my world. I still wonder what James witnessed at such a young age and how he must have tried to process it. I also wonder if our uncle raped him too, or attempted to. Had he made James do the same things as me? Did he force himself on James? I'm not really sure. Those answers were lost when James was murdered.

James from a very young age would always have four showers a day, sometimes more. No one was allowed to touch his soap, and he begin to wash his undies in the shower. He would have nightmares and didn't want to be left alone at night. People would often call James a mummy's boy; little did they know why. He would eventually grow out of the tantrums he would throw.

I would sometimes escape to other people's places where there would be some peace from the daunting events in our home, but whenever I went to our auntie and uncle's house, he would be at me. James told me about a time at the drive-in when they all went to the shop. I was left with our uncle. When they came back, he was kissing me passionately. My auntie said nothing; it was just expected.

As the years rolled past, the abuse went on, the rapes continued. It was the world that I lived in, a world without any sun, no windows to let light into the darkness surrounding me. My self-respect was gone. I had no self-esteem.

I was becoming more and more out of control. I would leave school and just wander. I would be called up to the headmistress and caned for leaving. My father's answer was to put me in an all-girls school. I played up so much at the interview that they didn't take me.

These torrid years were flying by, but not fast enough. I used to wonder what it was that we had done for our lives to be so fucked up. It's hard sometimes to put things in perspective. For such a long time, I thought the whole world was like this. It used to make me think that it wouldn't be great to come home to no fear, to really feel safe.

It got so bad that in high school, I began experimenting with boys on my own. I was having unprotected sex with lots of boys. Again, I was never told this was wrong, so how would I know? As I had been molested for such a long time, I thought that this was what went on. We didn't know about child molesters, and when the subject did come up, we were taught that it was strangers we had to look out for.

My world had taken on another dimension. Child abuse just wasn't spoken of. People were too scared to. I have to ask, are we afraid? Yes, I think we are. Why? Because child abuse is the most awful thing. It makes us question everything we hold dear. How can people we love hurt us so? Inside my own world was the most ugly, hideous place. I felt like my insides were oozing out, trying to get rid of the poison.

I remember quite clearly the last time he tried to touch me up. It was at my mum's. They had come to visit us. His wife went inside. I never really knew why, as Mum wasn't home. I told them that when they got out of the car. He lunged at me on the veranda and grabbed at my breasts. As I moved back, he reached for my body. I pushed his hand away and stepped back. I finally said, "No more!" I warned him that if he ever touched me again, I would tell my mum.

He laughed and said, "No one will listen. You are always in trouble. No one will care."

And yes, he was probably right. But in that moment, I had some control back. I knew then that he would leave me alone, and that was that.

It would be many years before our paths crossed again. My road to "who gives a fuck" was now on track. The difference between right and wrong, I didn't really know. Everything about my life had been a great big lie. Hiding the truth was the easy part; looking at and facing the truth seemed unbearable. So to lock it away as far back as I could possibly do was my mind's way of dealing with all the guilt and shame that I felt.

There are no words to describe how low I felt about myself because of the despicable things this man had done to me and the terrible things he made me participate in—not to mention what he had done to mine and my brother's mental state at the time. How do young children understand any of it? It's only now, as I've grown older, that I've tried working through and piecing together those terrible years.

Looking back, you see a pattern. I eventually used sex not so much for love—as that had never been shown to me or even told to me—but for control. That's what I believed and how I operated. I was never told that sex could be good or even be an act of love between two people. I sometimes hang my head in shame for some of the things that I have done, and even though I'm pretty hard on myself and I know that I have conquered these demons, it just sometimes sits in your gut, a feeling so bad. I had no respect for myself or anyone else.

It's amazing that two men who I thought loved me—one being my dad and the other my uncle—taught me nothing about love. What they taught me was that the female mind and body are worthless. It took many years for James and me to realize that we weren't to blame for the violence and sexual abuse against us. It took many years of therapy and self-examination, because sexual child abuse is the lowest of all acts, especially because it's against children who must come to terms with their innocence being robbed from them.

In time you begin to understand it's the molester who has the problem and not you. There are no valid excuses for these people. They take liberties that are not theirs to take. They take trust and love and treat them like they are worthless and dirty. They rob their victims of innocence and childhood.

What followed for James and myself were years of destruction. Our lives were out of control, without laws or boundaries, for there were never any for us to follow. It took years for me to find the courage to rid my life of these demons. As much as I believe I have dealt with them, there are still a few that I can't find the strength to truly face. I still feel ashamed in a strange sort of way. It's like part of you is dirty, and no amount of cleaning removes the grit that sits inside your soul.

After many years, most of my monsters have been put back where they belong. As for James, he was slowly coming to terms with his own sexual abuse and also coming to realize that he couldn't have helped me, as he was very young. His nightmares were horrifying for him, as he felt he had no control. So for James, control became very important.

He told me when he was about seventeen that he would become so big and mean that no one would ever hurt him again. He set off on a mission to become invincible. James was never one to let his guard down. This become more and more of an obsession with him. But sadly, he did let his guard down, just when for the first time in his life he was starting to ground himself and become a better person. It cost him his life.

When your trust has been so badly violated, it's hard to express yourself openly, as you are too scared that someone might see the vulnerable child who once was. How do you ever trust anyone again? That's the big question. One can only hope that in time, that will come back.

It's funny that it's sometimes not even the person you are with who you don't trust, it's yourself—too scared to let someone in, too scared to let someone get that close. In my life, most men I tried to trust eventually let me down. I know that unconditional love with another person is truly a wonderful thing, and I have that with my two children, but in a man–woman relationship, it doesn't exist. I know my wonderful husband feels it for me. There has always been hope, and that's what got me this far: hope and faith and courage that there are far more trustworthy people in the world than bad people. But it's what the bad people do that marks many people forever.

I could go on and on about this hideous crime, as it cuts so close to my heart and took precedence over many things in my life for a long time. That is coming to an end now thanks to my counsellor, who has helped me through the most turbulent events in my life. She has been a godsend, and my gratitude to her is endless. Besides the child abuse, she helped me deal with many other demons. For her, it was her job; for me, she was my light at the end of a tunnel in which I could only see blackness.

If you are lucky enough to find a good counsellor like I did, it's a step in the right direction, a forward step, as there are no more steps backward. You might be like me and have to go back to the bottom in order to lift yourself up. Dealing with child molestation takes all the courage you have.

As I mentioned earlier, the police charged my uncle with a number of offenses, including sexual misconduct when dealing with a child under the age of thirteen. This particular court case left me shaken from having to relive these horrible events over and over again. I remember thinking that this was a chance for my father to step up, but he was so fearful of secrets he just couldn't do it. He could not be a father. His own journey had many terrible secrets, and it was through knowing some of them that I knew how hard this trial would be.

My uncle refused to let his wife testify. He had bullied and manipulated other witnesses with their own dirty dark secrets, so they all lied in order to protect the other monsters. It was so sad that this was the code they lived by. It was devastating at the time. My brother drove down from the country where he worked to be by my side. He testified, but he just wasn't ready to face that particular demon. After the court case, I felt a sense of relief. Even though he was found not guilty, I knew that one day others would be brave enough to come forward, and I would be there for them.

Even though you face discrimination and are looked down on like it's your fault, rise above this and look inside. If you yourself are a victim or now a survivor, as I am, or even know someone who is being molested, listen with a loving heart, not a judgmental one. A quiet voice, not aggressive understanding, is hard unless you yourself have been through this hideous thing that you did not ask to be done to you. Don't be a judge. Be that unconditional love that does not reflect shame or guilt but gives a guiding hand. Sometimes that's the one thing a victim of sexual child abuse may need.

Abuse changed my life and my brother's life forever. Our road to self-destruction was easy. It was pulling up out of that spiral that was the hardest. Everyone deserves respect; everyone deserves the chance to be heard. Most of all, we all deserve not to have our childhood robbed and violated but to be able to feel and be safe with people we give our trust to. So sometimes, look behind the sad eyes and the need for approval. Remember that sometimes the lies become the truth, and the truth is a lie.

Look past your own vulnerability and be smart with your kids. I found my teenage years a nightmare straight from hell; this I would not wish upon anyone. I don't have many regrets in my life, as you can't change them anyway, but for the first twenty years of my life I had many understandings that this is what life threw at me. I think I got a bad deal, but even so, those things are what made me into the person I am today. They moulded me to be me.

I was judged according to what people saw. There was no hand to reach for me. I was a soul screaming for someone to help, and no help came. It made me think that this was truly how bad life was. I escaped the pain of my childhood by sleeping with many men, drinking, doing drugs—just anything to hide the pain that my world was in.

James also did things to escape. He did drugs and bashed people, and eventually he joined a bikie club. This was his way of concealing his pain: inflicting it upon other people through violence and control. He had no respect for women. He'd watched our mother put up with more abuse than anyone could imagine, and she stayed. He'd watched his sister be molested and raped, and she stayed. No matter what happened, we stayed. That's what a small boy saw. We did eventually leave, but the scars were already burnt into his mind.

There is hope; more and more doors are opening up for people who are caught in domestic violence and child sexual abuse. Schools, helplines, and government agencies are becoming more and more alert to these problems. So speak up and be heard. Don't be ashamed, be brave and fight back, with courage and faith for every step you take forward. You might fall back some, but the harder you push, the freer you become.

Remember, the shame and guilt are not yours, they belong to the person who has done this to you. Put the blame back where it belongs. Take the biggest breath of your life and believe that it will get better. It will take time and strength, for it drains your very soul, but in the end you will have taken the first step forward—the one that is the hardest.

Let the world judge the abusers and not their victims. Let all the unheard children be allowed to speak without fear. Do not turn away a hand that reaches for help and guidance. Do not judge something you don't understand or are too afraid to face, or you will give the molester the power to continue. Let the children be the winners. Let the adults who suffered these terrible things be believed. Give them back the self-worth that was taken without asking. Give the unheard voices the chance to be heard. Look for the signs. The truth doesn't come without pain, but the truth is the answer.

In some cases, the abuse is right in front of you. Sometimes people are blinded to what they see. Open your eyes and your heart and be true to yourself. Be true to the little people who God has entrusted to you. Be their voice.

As I close this chapter, it will always be a sadness in my life that words can't describe that our innocence was taken by this man, without permission from either of us. This robbery will always be a tragedy in our lives, but we can turn it around and do good with what we have. Child sexual abuse is a serious problem in all societies. It doesn't differentiate by colour or wealth. Society should make stronger laws to protect the innocent. Behind many closed doors are many closed eyes. Some people stay silent and do nothing because the truth is hard to face.

Those who sit and do nothing are also to blame for these terrible things that happen. When the questions come from your adult children, make sure you have answers they'll want to hear. Make the answers the right ones. Remember, be there to protect them, for they picked you as parents.

People go on about parents being overprotective. Myself, I don't see how it's better to prevent them. Sometimes the cure is too hard, and in some cases it just can't be reached. Allow your children to be safe and have good choices in their lives. Remember, you don't have to be rich in fortune to be rich in your life, for we are only given one life.

*It is during our darkest moments that we must focus to see the light.*
*—Aristotle*

# CHAPTER 3

## *Scams and Survival*

Fight or flight is an instinct that helps creatures survive in the most trying of times. We all want to live, we all want to have a say in our lives. We were all born the same way. But it's what comes after that makes us who we are. It's that word *hope* and our ability that gets us there in the end.

Survival is something we are taught, or somehow we find the ability just to get on with it. This sounds quite harsh, but I think when we are put in certain situations, we all want to live. I find when talking about criminal activity within our family, there is a great sense of remorse. It's not like we really ever wanted to steal, and by no means was it right, but this is how we did it. Our younger sister was the lucky one; she was brought up and lived in a different time.

My brother and I were shown and taught that stealing was the way to survive. My earliest memories are of my family being professional shoplifters. This ran on both sides of my family, so to blame one rather than the other is wrong. Shoplifting was a way of life for our aunties, and they were very good at what they did. Mum was also involved with this. There was never a shortage of new clothes for us to wear.

They would shoplift to order. This was an easy way of making money. One of my aunties was selling stolen suits to detectives on our police force. They would give her an order and she would fill it. it was mainly new suits that they wanted. I remember her favourite store for this was Men's Bits, a menswear store.

My other female auntie was the one who taught me how to steal, and even though I'm not proud of doing it, sometimes it was the only way to survive. When our parents split up, we were instantly poor. Even though Mum worked, she was paying a mortgage, and there wasn't enough money left for clothes or anything else.

I began by stealing clothes. I just wanted to try to fit in. All the kids at school would make fun of James and me because we were poor. I remember having only one pair of jeans, a couple of pairs of knickers, and no bras. Being constantly teased and bullied because you were poor, being called horrible names, can change your opinion of yourself. Not that I had much of an opinion.

After my parents separated and the molestation stopped, we learned to live a very different life. I wasn't stealing with my aunts anymore; it was a solitary thing. Sometimes I felt like people could see right through me to my damaged soul. I felt shame and guilt that had a life all of their own. My soul, or what was left of it, felt like it was drained of anything that might resemble goodness. It was open for all the world to judge. Not only would I be judged by my peers, but also by God. But being judged by people scared me more, as I knew God will forgive me.

I believed it was okay to do this, since my entire young life I had seen people taking what they wanted. When you're really poor, you can do the most terrible things. Crime and stealing were condoned in our family, so we always thought it was cool to scam, to do a job and find a sucker or a mark, as they're sometimes called. To be able to pull a job off was quite an achievement.

Whilst our parents were married, we had whatever we wanted, even though my father did not work. He managed to get money from somewhere. I think that's why it was so hard on us when they separated, because then we were reduced to a single-parent income. Make no mistake, my parents separating was the best thing ever. I would rather have a life of nothing than put up with what we did.

Our family made it look so very easy. There was a bit of talent that went into shoplifting in order not to be caught. We were always told, "Don't let an opportunity go by. Always look for the scam." I remember as small children, we would sit for hours watching and listening to how to put a scam together. It was like being taught how to butter a slice of bread. It was taught to us as a natural way of life.

As I mentioned in an earlier chapter, our father ran an illegal game. First he ran it in the bush. There would be people everywhere. As word went out on the grapevine, more and more people would come. People did not care that it was in the bush near the local dump. People would stand in the hot sun, on hot sand. There were large black flies all over the place. The smell was indescribable.

I'm not really sure how long he ran the game out there, but it was a while. The mixture of people ranged so much. There were people who just loved to bet, and people who were desperate to win some money, There were people with money, and there were poor people. There were always lots of people connected to the horse-racing industry. My father was also a part-time horse trainer for a while, and that was another industry that has always been marked as crooked.

Eventually the game was moved to our house. Our father would spend hours making dice tables, as they were always confiscated during the raids on our home. But if there was anything that this man could do in a hurry, it was make a dice table. Even as violent as he was, he was still our dad, and all children look up to their dad. Well, what image do you think we had of ours?

I remember him making baccarat shoes. It seemed he had found his scam and all the suckers he needed. There was never any shortage of people. He sent away for a machine that had come all the way from Japan. It helped him shave the dice, and then he would alter how many heads and tails were on it. They also fell a certain way. I would sit for hours helping him rub back the dice. Just being able to sit quietly with this man was a feat in itself. Whilst he was working on his gaming tools, he was calm.

He would paint pennies with a lead paint so they fell the way he wanted. We would practice for hours with him. I think this was probably one of the very few times we spent playing with our father There was always plenty to do, and my father liked to give the impression that we were doing okay financially.

I remember the raids on our house. The police would come and see him a week or so beforehand. These were detectives, as they were not in uniform. They would discuss when they would come, and what time they would be there. This was so he wouldn't have bookmakers there or any off-duty police or politicians—people of good standing in our community.

I remember standing at the door when they came. I was always curious about the police. My dad would hand them an envelope with money in it. I used to say, "How come you give them money, Dad?"

He would shrug and reply, "That's their wages. Everyone has to be paid." They all seemed to love playing cloak-and-dagger.

He made more money in those short years than he made in his whole life. Not that it lasted long, as he also had a very bad gambling problem. Whatever he won would eventually end up at the illegal gambling places in town. They were run by the Italians at that time. He would always go to either Spirals or Franks. They had set up their clubs in town. These were fitted out quite stylishly. The clubs were very popular, but they would only allow men in. Our father allowed women as well at his games, because he found that they loved to gamble just as much.

Trainers, jockeys, owners, strappers, track riders, stable hands, blacksmiths, bookmakers, jewellers, stockbrokers, politicians, business owners, madams, prostitutes, gangsters, police officers, drug dealers, smugglers—the picture I'm trying to put into your head is that criminals from all parts were never far from our lives. Some of them seemed really nice. They would often tell James and me stories of their great conquests. We would be left in awe at story after story. Some were mind-blowing, especially since we were very young and impressionable.

James was always interested in hearing all the gory details. Not me; I think I'd seen enough. But James just loved hearing about guns and shootings. Crime was never an illegal activity, it was a way of life. There were members of our immediate family who were hardened criminals. We had another uncle who used to belong to the notoriously violent gang called Jaw Breakers. He served a great deal of time in prison for various crimes. I was even told he was a hit man and had done about fifteen years for murder.

For people who are scratching their heads about what the hell I'm talking about, the Jaw Breakers were a gang of horrible men who brutalized and terrorized. They bashed people in order to get protection money. They ran illegal prostitution in their local area. The theme was that they would break people's jaws; this was their trademark. They were feared in their local area, and interstate people were often too scared to even talk about them.

I did not really think much of our jaw-breaking uncle, but he was always good to James. He was not a big man in stature but a slender man. I used to think his face was sad. He never really ever looked happy. He gave my aunt a terrible time in the early days; he was also a wife-basher. He had a wandering eye as well.

Another close friend of our father's was in the notorious Italian Mafia. He was another one who had done serious time. I was told he also was a hitman in his day. He was just so awful, I truly was terrified of him.

The Mafia controlled all of the underworld. I remember John—that was his name—was a tallish man with an big ego. He was a real tough character. I never really liked him or his stories, as he really scared me. My brother James always liked to listen to the stories, as John made them sound so exciting. My father would tell me that if I backchatted John, he would take me away and cut me up. I was very scared. The Mafia made headlines all over the world with their violence and lack of respect for the law.

These men were not to be fucked around with. They were the real deal, really bad men. These were criminals who had no morals. They were extremely ruthless.

I remember James telling me that they had told him about people they had killed. It was pretty sick, not just the killings but bragging to children about it. No wonder James thought violence was great. His father used it to beat up on a woman, and these men used it as a way of life.

Don't get me wrong; I listened too. We had stories told to us by smugglers, horse-dopers, and any other petty criminal who was allowed into our home. We would sit for hours and listen and just take it all in. This was probably the only time our father wasn't angry at the world. James and I still loved our dad.

The game at the house was always packed on the weekends. That is why we were sometimes sent to our relatives. During the week it wasn't as busy, but our father would often be in town at the other clubs. On arriving home from school, we'd find our home full of people. Our parents would put out snacks. Drinks were also provided. Our father's theory was, "keep them happy and they will come back." It didn't matter that they lost lots of money.

My father did very well early on with the game. Our parents owned their own home fairly young. Mum made sure that the house was paid for, so whilst they were together, our material life was fine. They still shoplifted, but not as much in these particular years. But our father blew whatever money was left. This went on for many years. The police taking money from my father were part of different investigations for police corruption and even murder. One was even killed in a shoot-out that bikies were involved with. This was a terrible thing, as an innocent man was killed as well.

When I look back at some of those police officers, I think they were more dangerous than some of the gangsters we had in our lives. They could break the law but also hide behind it and use it to their advantage when they needed to. Our gangster friend would tell me and James that to face your enemy was the right thing to do. Don't cower; don't be the lesser man. Look your enemy in the eye—before shooting or bashing them, I presume he meant. James always did that that, I will say. When he bashed people, they knew it was him. He never took the easy way out. He was always the man who wasn't afraid. This was one piece of advice that he followed.

When we got raided, it was always organized. A bus would pull up in our street, and a floodlight would light up our home like daylight. It was like a movie set, but the director was a police officer. People would scramble; they would be jumping fences and running everywhere. It was pure chaos. Many times, men would run into the house to escape. They would hide in our beds or our bedrooms so they wouldn't be caught. It was not unusual to wake up with someone next to me.

It was only a small fine that my parents would get. Our father would always pay in order to keep the authorities happy, but it was an inconvenience most of all because they would have to get on the bus and go downtown.

We would have leading jockeys at our home from Friday night until they were ready to go to the races and ride on Saturdays. Many times trainers would ring looking for there "hoops" (jockeys), as the game would continue all night. They would go ride, and then they would be back again as soon as the races were finished.

The number of scams that were organized at our home was mind-blowing, from pulling up horses to drugging them to bird smuggling.

Prostitution rackets, stand-over people, you name it, we saw it. Men were bashed at our home whilst we were there. We would see men beaten for whatever reason. Our kitchen would be covered in blood or our back veranda, and people never really seemed to be bothered by it. There was really very little reaction from anyone. The only thing I recall is that the basher would have to get someone to clean up the mess.

James and I wouldn't get very worried about it. It was probably like our mother getting bashed—it was just the way things seemed to be. I could only imagine that James thought this was how you deal with people: you either bash them or you intimidate them to do what you want them to do. This was a normal thing to us.

Many a night I would wake up and our father would be stuffing money into my pillowcase. My room was at the back part of the house. I would mostly sneak into James's room, as his room was at the front. We would often sleep together, either because it was too noisy at the back or just for comfort after watching our father beat our mother. He would often beat her, I think, so that he would have an excuse to leave the house and go gamble.

Gambling is such a terrible disease. Our father lost so much money, it is mind-blowing. James never really ever got into gambling; he was so determined not to be like our father. Growing up, the idea that there was nothing wrong with crime was embedded in our small minds. Somehow our destiny was changed from when we were born. The imprints of our childhood were embedded. We didn't have a choice, or so we thought. It's only as you grow that you realize there is a choice you can make. Changing a chapter in one's life is just like turning a page in a book.

I don't really think our father ever experienced any real emotion. At times, it seemed as though he had no soul. If our father lost money at either club, he would send out his gossips to inform people of a game being started up earlier. These games were just feeding his addiction to gambling.

Our father even put a plan together to rob the place in town he himself had been barred from for cheating. Yeah, he got caught. I think they thrashed him and barred him for life. The Italians did not take kindly to being robbed, so he devised a plan to get himself back in. One of the clubs was holding a ladies' night where men and women could go. So his scam was to dress as a woman. He dressed himself up, shaved his legs and arms, and put on a wig, make up, and a dress.

First, though, he needed to see if he could really pass, so he was dropped of into town to see if he could get picked up. Bingo! He was. He found himself at Kings Park with a man who had picked him up. He got himself in a compromising situation. He finally got away from the man, so the scam was on.

His best friend at the time, a man called Harry, was to also be at the club, but as himself. Mum and another lady went as well. Mum said they spent hours putting on all the make-up and getting our father ready for his sting. He just wanted to rob the Italians. In they marched with not even a blink. Our father had his crooked dice with him. He started to play slowly at first, then he switched the dice. He gave Mum the dice he had lifted to get rid of. She went into the toilet and put them in the toilet tank.

Now for the sting. These were head dice, as our father mostly backed heads. They started off slowly so as to draw no suspicion to themselves. The night was going according to plan … well, at least they thought it was. Suddenly, the owner and a couple of his heavies walked over to the table and asked our father about his betting.

Mum and the other lady saw there was trouble and tried to walk out, but they were stopped. Our father and Henry were asked to escort them into the office, as the owner wished to have a word. Mum and the other woman were released, but our father and Henry were made to undress. Even though the Italians had their suspicions that something was amiss, I think they were shocked when they realized our father was actually a man dressed as a woman.

The owner had removed the dice from the table and was now looking for the other set. They had the crooked dice but no real proof that it was our father and Henry who had made the switch. Our father and Henry pleaded their innocence, saying he was only dressed as a woman because he had been previously barred. "It could have been anybody!" they cried. "We just picked the dice from the basket."

They were bashed up and made clear examples of what would happen to anyone caught robbing the place again. They were actually lucky they weren't shot. They were warned not to ever set foot in the place again or they would face serious consequences. They would not be so lucky next time.

The owners took all the money that our father and Henry had won, so they were left with nothing but a few bruises as a reminder. It was a real joke for a while, but the Italian gents were not very impressed, and it was widely known that our father would never be allowed back. The Italians did not take kindly to being a joke.

Our father finally decided to move his game from our home and opened a place in a small port town. It was done very nicely. He spent money to get it how he wanted it to look, creating a gambling palace. I suppose he wanted to show the Italians they could not have it all their way. The game was going well, and he was making money again.

He was good friends with a young TV journalist The journalist himself was good friends with a legendary journalist. They decided to make a documentary called *No Demons No More*. It was half about the running of illegal games and half about a former prostitute who had been murdered. It amazes me that all these things intertwined somehow. It must be because some of these people were the lowest form of scum. No killer was ever caught. Her body was found in her car at a nearby rubbish tip. It was always rumoured that a former high-ranking policeman was the one who shot her. The gossip was that she had too much dirt on police officers and politicians, and it was presumed she was using her knowledge to blackmail them.

The documentary was filmed in our back shed. I think Channel 9 still has a copy of this in its archives. I inquired once about it, and to the best of my knowledge, it's there.

The scams continued at our father's gaming place. More fools would come. Our father was in his element. He was finally running a gambling establishment equal to that of his Italian friends.

Our father was now looking for different ways to scam. He and an associate who was a leading trainer at the time decided to try bird smuggling, as there was a real market for them overseas, especially in Asia, where there were rich Asians willing to pay huge amounts of money for birds. Parrots were mostly what they were after. So a special cage was made to house the birds. Our father worked on this forever. They had to be just right. Special packaging was made to hold each bird. Once the birds were drugged, they were put into the packaging and cases. Birds were also strapped onto the runner. Time was the problem, as the birds had to be drugged for a while in order to keep them quiet.

They did a few dummy runs in order to get it right. The runners were put on planes and sent to different destinations. It was important to work out how much drug was to be given to the birds. Also, a contributing factor was plane pressure. Would the cases be okay? Would the birds survive?

They got a few runs through, but they needed to work out how many they could fit into cases. Birds had to be caught in nets up north, so trips to the north to trap were inevitable. They would set up huge nets to catch the birds. The really expensive ones were stolen from various aviaries around town They were even stolen from people's homes just to get the numbers up. They made load of trips to Asia; they would employ runners a bit like the early drug runners, but they weren't smuggling drugs, it was birds.

They did come undone sometimes when either they were searched or birds would suddenly wake up and start squawking. Our house was raided, and birds were confiscated. We were never far from the police, whether they were there to sort out the domestic problems or the scams. I recall our father being caught once in Asia.

Our father was getting more and more involved in the criminal world. Horse-training had taken a back seat. He had been warned by the Turf Club to cease his gaming, but there was more money to be made from it than the training of horses. Not to leave the horse-racing industry out of it; there were scams pulled with gallopers and trotters, as our father had friends in both of these industries and there was money to be made. Horses were often drugged and backed off the boards. Jockeys were paid to pull up horses. The trots were easier to get a horse beat.

As time went on, our father's involvement with the drugging of horses would prove to have great possibilities. The track-horse scams seemed easier for a while. A drug had been found called tiger serum. This drug was tested on different horses to get the right result. As horses could have heart attacks if given too much, the gallopers were hit. The stewards knew there was a real problem with this drug. Jockeys and trainers were all involved, as the bookmakers were the target. And so the sting would begin. Finally the stewards were getting on top of the problem with raids on houses. Premises were searched. There were a few people who went down for this.

The trots were also a huge target. On one occasion, a well-known trotting driver and a well-known race caller were involved with the drugging of trotters. On one night, two horses were given the drug. It was going to be a huge win, but the trotting driver that was involved licked the spoon after the horse was administered the drug, and he nearly died. They decided to try to walk it off him. Meanwhile, the horses were on the track. The race caller told them to leave the driver, as he was panicking, thinking he was going to die. They actually never made it to the track to back the horses. They both won at huge odds, but the elephant-juice scandal was all about, so the chances of getting another hit at it were getting unlikely.

The race caller and driver were known to be involved with heavy drugs. It would be their final undoing in the industry that they both loved. The driver had had the world at his feet, as he himself had driven many a good horse home. He was the golden boy—another story of how the fall from grace can be harsh.

Our father never really got into that drug scene, as it didn't interest him. But the scams went on and on. He was no longer really involved with our everyday lives because of all the scams and robbing of people. Our father was also good to many people. In an industry veiled by glamour, there are many poor people struggling to survive. Our parents fed, clothed, and loaned more people money. There was always someone with a hard-luck story to tell us.

We were brought up not thinking anything was wrong with scamming someone, as crime was never discussed as bad but just a way of making a quick buck. The life of elite crime seemed to outshine anything else that was real in our lives. It had been part of our whole life. They say crime doesn't pay, but it always paid our bills.

My brother's world became somewhat different from mine. His criminal activity was more sinister. I got to see the darker side of crime through him, and the consequences through his many experiences with the justice system, both before and after his death. My own frustrating court experiences involved family-law court. Although it is a digression from the story of our childhood, I'll tell you my family-law court story here, since it illustrates how patterns of violence have been repeated in my life, and how the law is still failing to protect children at risk.

The family-law court is a place where devils are in control, a place without a heart. No wonder so many people get angry. I fought in the family-law court for about ten years against my children's father. At one point, I did have a lawyer, but after many years and about a hundred thousand dollars, I could not afford a lawyer anymore.

I tried to protect my children from a man who I believed had few morals. Yes, I did have two children with him and knew bits of his past. I knew he had been to prison for drugs. I really did think he would change, but leopards never change their spots, they just hide them for a while.

After he slapped me across the face when I was four months pregnant, I left. Then the ugly past started to creep in. He came to my home and smashed up the front with a crowbar. I was scared out of my wits.

Fortunately, the children were at my mum's. But when he realized the children weren't there, he sped around to her house. My children were only seven months old and two-and-a-half years at the time. I rang Mum and told her, "I think he's coming. Ring the police." But every time my mum tried to contact the police, she was put on hold.

I eventually got to my mum's, where he was out front. He was like a crazy man. *God*, I thought, *I cannot go through this again. I will not put my children through what I went through and witnessed.*

He was smashing my mum's windows. Mum had my baby son in her arms and my small girl at her feet. The children were screaming. The police were taking too long. Mum decided to call out to her side neighbour to come and get my children.

I was pleading with him to stop. He ran at my car and threw the crowbar at the window. It smashed the window and narrowly missed my head. I took off and turned around. There was a family down the street. I screamed to them to call the police.

He got into his car to follow me. My heart was racing. I was shaking so much I could not think. I was so scared and did not know what to do.

My brother was living down the road at that time, but when I pulled up at the crossroad, I could not turn right. There were too many cars. He was right behind me. I decided to turn left. I sped off, hoping all the while to get away from him. I could see him in my rear-vision mirror. He had now turned the same way as me. My heart nearly jumped clean out of my chest.

I was speeding to get away. The next minute, *bam bam*, he rammed my car. *Bam bam* again. I could not think. The car was all over the place. The next minute he rammed me again, this time hooking onto my car. I had no control. I was terrified. He drove even faster. I could not break free.

The next minute, he pushed my car into the curb at a huge force. I could see a bus stop coming. *My God*, I thought, *I'm going to hit it!* I braced myself. My body went tense. I had my hand so tight on the steering wheel. At the last minute, my car broke loose from his. I came to a sudden stop, narrowly missing the concrete bus shelter. I sat there for a moment as he sped off.

Once I regained my composure, my mum and kids were all I could think of. I reversed to get out of the ditch, and I got back onto the road. I was so scared he was going to come back. I pulled up outside my mum's neighbour's house, banging on the door. They let me in. Mum was at the fence, and I raced to meet her.

The neighbour got me a chair. I reached over. My baby son was screaming; he was shaking. I got hold of him and passed him to the neighbour. I reached over and grabbed my daughter. She was hanging on like grim death, crying and screaming.

Mum was devastated. We could hear cars passing. With every sound, we thought it was him coming back. Terrified for our lives, I hid the kids with my mum's neighbours. I crept around the front of the yard, making sure he was nowhere in sight. I looked at the damage he had done to the front of my mum's house. It was just awful. How could he do this? My mum was still shaking. She told me it brought back terrible memories for her. She was sobbing.

The next minute, my brother pulled up with the police. One of the neighbours had rang him. James was so angry, he was yelling at the police, asking, "What took you so long? Someone could have been killed." To me, he said, "Where is he?"

"I don't know," I blurted out.

"Where are the kids?" James asked.

"There, next door."

"Right," he said.

The police looked at the mess at my mum's house. Then I went with them to my home to show them what he had done. Whilst we were there, he rang. He was so calm he was scary. He told me to tell the police that he was at his house. "Tell them they can come get me."

He was charged with a number of offences for this episode. So whilst the family-law court gave me a hard time again, I was protecting my babies. Justice Money was the judge I had the most problem with. Every time we went into court, I would simply disobey her order. "I was right," I would tell her. But she insisted that he should be allowed to see the children. She kept at me. I kept on telling her that the family-law court is stagnant. They assume that all people are round pegs. I told her I was a square peg; I would simply not yield.

This went on for years, until one day she threatened me. She put me in a situation where there was no way out. I had to yield. He saw my children under supervision for the next eight years. At least there would always be someone else with them.

Eventually we went back into court again. I was still fighting to protect my children We ended up getting a new judge: the head judge, Judge Curner. We were heading into trial, and for as long I had the ability, I would stand in front of that judge and argue the point. I had only done it for short periods of time in the past. This time we had a three-day trial where I would have to ask witnesses questions, cross-examine them, and put my best case forward. I had homework to do. I just got into it; no point procrastinating. We were headed for trial.

The day arrived. I was very nervous, but I relied on the fact that he had records for drugs and violence After three days of trial, I was very proud of myself. I conducted myself very well. The council for the children was a stern woman, and I did not get along with her. I believe she hated women and was all for the man. She made my life hell.

In closing, I told Judge Curner and his lawyer and the children's lawyer that he would reoffend. I was shot down. They told me I was being stubborn and had tunnel vision. *Yeah*, I thought. Well, the judge made the ruling that he was allowed to see the children unsupervised. They told me again I was wrong and that he had learned his lessons and would not reoffend. *Yeah right*.

Guess what? Three years later, he was back in court, charged with more drug offences. One year after that, he was back in prison. I decided to write to the family-law court and the other two lawyers and vent my anger, explaining to them that I was right. Sometimes I think people take the view that people change. Some might; some do not.

I do not believe that my view was heard. The family-law court works under this holy grail—that it is the child's best interest that matters most—yet after time, you come to realize that the system is not fair. I was willing to fight to the end. I believed that I was right. Always be true to yourself and to your children.

If the only reason you don't want your children to see the other party is because you are angry and vengeful over your relationship breaking down, then you really need to look inside of yourself. When you can clearly see the right answer, you will be true to yourself and to your children.

In finishing this chapter, I reflect that even as you get older and wiser, so to speak, the world of crime or courts is not for the faint-hearted. Sometimes the consequences are far too great. To live by the sword is no easy task.

*Experience is not what happens to you;*
*it's what you do with what happens to you.*
*—Aldous Huxley*

# CHAPTER 4

## *Running from the Truth*

Truth. Well, there's a word that comes in many forms, but it's within the boundaries of our conscience where we find our own. Some people's truth is their journey, or it can be an expansion of what we try to justify.

This part of my book describes many mistakes I have made along the way. There is no point in regretting everything one does, no matter how bad. It's only bad if you don't learn from it all, and let me assure you, I'm still learning from the many things in my life that made little sense. These years were a blur for a while. It took many years of therapy to understand my destructive behaviour, but even through it all, I feel that this was part of my journey. Unfortunately, many more problems occurred along the way. But again, it was only a chapter in my life.

As our mother settled into a new life without our father, she started working full-time as a cook. I was left to deal with responsibilities that should never have been mine. I was thirteen and James was nine. Mum would often work late at the hotel. I was to cook, clean, look after James, and try to understand what the fuck was wrong with me.

My parents' life was so fucked up. Mum was now seeing a man ten years her junior. He would be our sister's father. I did not like him much, from the very start. He was a drunk. I never understood Mum's attraction to him, as she hated alcohol. She never drank and despised our father's drinking, but here we were again with another man who was a very heavy drinker and so immature.

He and his friends would be at our home on the weekends, partying, drinking, drugging. It seemed to never end. I hated being there. The time she spent at work or with him gave me free time, though, and left me to my own devices—which weren't good. My screwed-up childhood was now taking its toll on me.

I was running from anything and everything to escape the terrible pain and turmoil I found myself in. I started sleeping with boys, drinking, and occasionally doing pot—anything to dull these memories, anything to dull the pain that I was in. Realizing what my uncle had been doing sent my world into chaos. I had no one to talk to. I found the whole thing overwhelming, to say the least. The memories were haunting. I just wanted them to stop, to go away.

Mum had a great bar at home. She supplied it for her boyfriend and his friends, so getting alcohol was easy. It was right at my fingertips. The first boy I slept with, I told him I was a virgin, as I was too embarrassed to say anything else. The first time, my friends told me, hurts like hell. With this in mind, I lied even more, as I experienced no pain.

The endless messes I got myself in were unbelievable. Never knowing how to say no, I slept with many young men. Mind you, I was only fourteen at the time. I was so determined to forget what had happened to me that I pushed it as far back as I could, living a life quite out of control. Mum seemed too busy to see what was going on. Her boyfriend moved in, and I despised him more and more. James hated him so much. He use to beat James up and torment him endlessly whilst she wasn't home.

I just looked for excuses not to be home. I was off doing anything to help stop the pain. These years were extremely hard for James and me, as so much had gone on in our lives up to that date. There never seemed to be any peace.

My world was filled with so many emotions. I had hormones running through my body that I didn't understand. Mum had never explained anything to James or me about sex or drugs or alcohol. When I got my period at age eleven, I thought I was dying, as I had never been told anything. Talking your kids and explaining the facts of life can only benefit them. How I never got pregnant at such a young age is a miracle. Maybe God looked out for me, as that road would have been harder.

My young teenage years were spent wagging school, smoking, drinking, and having unprotected sex. I was labelled a hell-raiser in my early years, which I think was probably unfair, as all the boys I knew could sleep with whomever they wanted. That stigma still exists today. They say we are equal; well, that is still yet to be proven.

I was attending nightclubs at fifteen. I had older friends, so I used to use their IDs to get in. Drugs were something that I really never got into. Pot was always popular, and I could handle that. I tried trips, but they sent me into a world that I had no control over, and I needed to feel in control. I knew what it was like to have no control over things that were done to me. I had to have control over my own life.

To me, that meant sleeping with anyone I fancied. There were many lovers. I suspect they always thought that I was a conquest, but in most cases sleeping with them was a victory for me. Well, at least that's what I thought. When I look back now, I see things differently. We are always clever in hindsight. I think it comes with maturity and finding that the ground you are standing on has finally stopped moving.

Having no boundaries in our lives, we set our own agenda. I was a party girl. Oh, I did have a steady boyfriend who is even today my very best friend, but he was also out sowing his wild oats, so my thought was, *Why can't I?* No one had ever told me that it just wasn't really the done thing. So off I went. I did as I pleased.

Mum did try, I think, to pull me into line, but it all came too late. With her working at the hotel, James and I spent quite a lot of time on our own. Even when she was there, her time was spent with her boyfriend. I learned to run a house. I took care of James if I was there. If not, James would often spend his time at his mate's place. James had been friends with him right through those years. The only thing I begrudge is that it seemed my entire childhood had been taken from me, and I couldn't do a damn thing about it.

Mum got a day job for a while at a bakery, delivering bread. On some occasions I would go and help Mum on her run. Most times, I was dog-tired, as I'd been out all night. We would deliver bread to shops and homes. Mum would get me to count bread that was left over in the shops. Most times I would get it right.

This one shop always used to annoy the crap out of me. He would have crates of bread left mostly unsliced. Mum would tell me to hurry up, so in the end, I would just guess, and Mum would write it in her book. Well, bugga me, the shopkeeper also had written it down, and the amount I gave my mum and his did not match. We never stole it. Good God, who would want unsliced bread? Sadly, though, Mum got called into her head office, and she was to be charged for stealing a hundred loaves of unsliced bread. Mum tried to explain to them that it was a mistake, but she should not have had me on her run, so they did not care. Mum pleaded guilty to the hundred loaves just because it was a joke. No one cared that it was my fault. Mum was fined a hundred dollars.

During this same period of time, Mum had bought a second-hand car from a car yard. She owed them five hundred dollars. She brought me with her to the car yard, and as we pulled up, Mum handed me the money and told me to go into the office and ask for the car salesmen. I found the salesman and gave him the money. I didn't know I was supposed to get a receipt, so out I walked. Mum assumed they would send the receipt.

A few months went by, and the police called around. They asked Mum to go with them to the police station. They needed her to answer some questions. As usual, I was out and about. When I got home, Mum said, "We have to go the police station tomorrow."

I looked at her and asked, "Why? What's going on?"

Mum said, "Remember a few months ago, I got you to give that car salesman the money?"

"Yeah," I answered.

"Well, apparently he did not hand it over, and now they say I owe them five hundred dollars."

"Mum," I answered, "but I did give it to him!"

Oh well. The next day Mum drove me over to the police station. I must admit, at fifteen it kind of intimidated me. I had butterflies racing around my tummy. I started to shake and get real nervous.

It would have been just great to be able to be kids without all the crap that went on in our world. Such a small thing to ask for. My learned behaviour was now taking hold. For years I saw that no one else followed the rules, so they must not apply to me either. I really had no respect for myself or anyone else. My self-esteem had taken a terrible battering. I found it easier to be out of control. It felt normal to me. James spent the majority of the time out of control as well; we just did different things in order to cope.

Sex, to me, was about control, as that was a learned pattern. My uncle had control over me, so as I turned the situation around, men became my victims. They were easy, as sex was a tool. My sexual experience shocked some, as I was still very young. Amazing how many men want to sleep with young girls. Going for older men meant they always supplied the drink or drugs, so it worked out to be a double bonus.

I was staying out at night. Mum found me a couple of times at a pub drinking with my friends. Mind you, most of us were underage, but each time you get caught you get smarter. I look back at some of the stupid things I allowed myself to do. Hitch-hiking was something everyone did. There was never any fear of being raped or murdered. As time marched on, I hated being at home. James was suffering terrible things from our mum's boyfriend, and I couldn't help him. It was easier to just not be there.

I finally had enough being suspended from school for shocking behaviour. Getting the cane was something that was normal. I expected to get it at least once a week. My behaviour at school was a such a problem that leaving and getting a job seemed the better idea. So at age fifteen, I left school.

Our father got me a job with a trainer he had been working with. Our father was living on the property when I first got there, but he eventually disappeared. I was only fifteen, and there were no adults in charge of me. What a way to go, doing as I pleased. When I look back now, it was a serious cry for help, but there was no one to hear it. My bad behaviour looked like rebellion, and maybe some of it was, but I just wanted someone to care. It didn't matter who it was.

As I was left alone there on the property, I was very popular with the young apprentices who worked with me. I slept with at least two of them. They were both young as well. This situation didn't last very long, as the novelty was wearing off. I just wanted someone to be there for me. I was desperate for someone to love me, and love me for something other than sex. I really didn't know what I was doing. I was a child inside a body that had been made a woman's earlier than it should have been.

The pay for the job was terrible. I was earning about thirty dollars a week and had to buy my own food. I ended up becoming so thin it was shocking. I would go home to see Mum and James on my weekends off. I really did miss them so very much, but I just wanted to be free.

James used to compete in BMX racing, something he became very good at. He also was right into motorbike riding. He had a trail bike that he and his mates would ride at the bunter—a large area of vacant land with a small river through it perfect for motorbike riding. James was really good at trail riding. He had his first motorbike at four; it was called a road-hopper. He seemed to find peace out on the dirt.

Mum had moved closer to her own mum and dad in order to stop our father from the continuous harassment. This actually worked. I can't ever recall him being violent in that house. But he moved into a flat not that far away.

Mum would come and pick me up on Sundays so I could spend time with my family. She would always comment on how thin I was, but I brushed it off. James would tell me what he had been up to. Sometimes he would ride his bike up to our father's flat to see him. Our father would ring Mum and tell her to come and get him, that he didn't have any time for us. I learned early that our father was only ever nice for his own reasons. There would always be a hidden motive, mostly to be able to get closer to Mum.

I eventually had enough of working on the farm and moved back home. I was transferred to another stable, which I really hated. I was working for another villain. It was like, *Are there any nice people left?* I'm sure there were, just not in my world, not then.

I got another job. A friend I had made in high school was also living at my mum's, and we moved into a flat not far from Mum and James. I was about seventeen now and thinking I was in control of my own life. My rules, finally. I was earning money to pay the rent. James and his mates would come visit. My only regret is that I never took James with me to live, but my own life was so fucked up that I don't think it would have worked.

James was now having a terrible time. Mum's boyfriend was beating him more and more. James used to come and tell me Mum's boyfriend would humiliate him in front of his friends constantly. Mum never seemed to see any of it, I'm not really sure why.

A few months later, Mum's boyfriend was jailed for a few minor offences. He had gotten picked up for drunk driving and gave his younger brother's name. The police somehow realized he was lying. They were both charged with conspiracy.

Mum's boyfriend was jailed for seven years. He was sent to a notorious prison. This was what real jail was about. He would tell us how horrible it was. There were no toilets in the cells, only buckets. Most times, you shared a cell. The rapes and bashings were somehow overlooked. He told us it was the most terrifying time of his life. His brother had gotten off with a good-behaviour bond. Lucky him.

This left Mum in a terrible situation, as there was no money. I moved back home for a little while to help out. James was working part-time. He eventually left school in order to get a full-time job. He worked with our uncles in the roof-tiling industry. These people also made James's life really hard. They would constantly torment, humiliate, and just be so mean to him.

James stuck it out. He was a hard worker. We both just didn't want to be poor. Whilst Mum's boyfriend was in jail, it was terrible. His younger brother moved in to help out. We would all go to work to help out.

Mum got pregnant with our sister whilst her boyfriend was in jail. On the prison farms, the prison officers were a bit more relaxed, so anything was possible. People would often smuggle in alcohol, drugs, or even be able to have sex with their woman. It was not a foolproof system, or I don't think so, anyway.

This made things a bit harder, as Mum wasn't working. She would be up there visiting him a couple of times a week. Still, it gave James some peace for a while. I was eighteen and James was fourteen when our sister was born. She was a welcome sight and brought joy into our lives. Her birth was just amazing. This beautiful little person brought hope back into our lives.

Mum's boyfriend had been released from prison just prior to our sister's birth. So I moved back out again. I just couldn't stand him. James was becoming more and more rebellious as he was growing up, but the constant badgering from Mum's boyfriend was taking its toll.

I remember one of our cousins staying over. James was very close to him; they were the same age. Mum's boyfriend caught them trying to light up a smoke, so for punishment, he made them each smoke a pack of cigars. Both boys became violently ill, and they never smoked again. He was sadistic in his punishment of James. He would get right off on hurting him.

Unfortunately, our young cousin got killed at seventeen. He was run over by a steamroller. This shattered our family. James never really got over losing him. I remember one time, James said he was awakened by our cousin's presence in his room. Our cousin had come to tell James it wasn't his time yet. He told James he would be waiting for him when it was his time. James was quite shaken over the whole thing.

Our sister was about two months old when I found myself pregnant. I was terrified. I had nothing, and my life was in such a state that thinking clearly about it just didn't seem possible. The boy I had been seeing for a while was the father. He had just told me that he had gotten another girl pregnant. I was shattered. I hadn't even told him at that point. Finally, I summoned up the courage to tell him. He went ballistic and pushed me around, screaming at me that he wasn't able to cope with the situation. I was crying and scared, because for the first time in a while, I was truly out of control.

I rang my mother to tell her about the fight I'd had with him. She told me she couldn't talk, as she was at work. I was shattered, standing there feeling very much alone. I went into my room and just sobbed my heart out.

The next day, I went over to Mum's to talk to her about the pregnancy. My nana was also there. They began to tell me how hard it would be, as I was only eighteen. I sat there and listened; they were the older ones, and I was hoping for a bit of advice. I was shattered as the cruel reality became obvious: I would have to terminate the baby or have it and adopt it out. Neither really appealed to me, but I felt I had no support. The lecture went on and on.

I think now if there had been a positive that they could make me see, I would have kept the baby. I really wanted to, but I was so scared. Thinking about taking care of someone else terrified me to no end, as I found it hard most times to take care of myself.

I remember thinking, *God, how cruel can life be?* The baby, I thought, would at least love me, although the kind of love I was used to was not a good thing. Sex was always part of that, and I remember thinking, *What if something so awful would happen to the baby?*

Mum and Nana went on and on about all the disadvantages this would bring to my very mixed-up life. I went ahead and arranged the termination. I recall going to the surgery, and the doctor and nurse sat down with me and explained what the procedure was, not that it made any sense to me. I was a mess. I sat there sobbing, the tears rolling down my face, and their voices seemed to fade. They kept asking me if I was sure this was what I really wanted. I still couldn't speak; I just sat there shaking my head. My heart was breaking. I felt like I was killing part of myself.

I was in a situation that I should have never been in, and having to decide such a thing tore my insides out. My termination was set for the next day. The doctor was quite surprised that I even came back. I sat there all alone. No one came with me. It was always the same. It was something that I got used to, not something that I really wanted in my life.

When they called my name, I was so distressed. They gave me something to calm me down before they put me under. I was right at thirteen weeks, so I had left it as long as possible. The operation went ahead, as I felt I had no choice. When I awoke from the operation, I was in a little cubicle by myself. I just lay there sobbing and in so much pain emotionally. My life seemed more mixed-up than ever.

They eventually rang Mum to come and get me. She drove me home to where I was living. I went straight to bed. I remember locking my door and just sitting there crying like never before. Again, I felt something had been taken away from me. I felt I had no control. My life got worse for a while, as I began to punish myself for the terrible thing I had done.

I was working two jobs. I would go from one to the other, and then we would party all night. I was drinking all the time and taking party drugs as a way to dull the pain. I always felt like I was in nothing. My life seemed normal. The boy I had gotten pregnant by had been sleeping around continuously. The other girl he had gotten pregnant had just given birth to a girl. I was devastated. We stayed together—why, I'm not sure, as he was sleeping with anybody or anything.

So I decided again to hit the nightclub scene. It had been a way of life for me forever, so being there and being out of control was like being home. It was where I felt comfortable. There were always people I knew there, and we would just go on for days. I never missed work; I always went, as without money, you couldn't party.

The number of men I slept with amazed even myself. With all those men, I only ever slept with one married man. Was I ashamed? Yes, very much so. He was having difficulties in his marriage, and I had just come out of a three-year relationship. My life was tumbling again, out of control, back to where it felt right. I'd seen the many men in my life as conquests, but this married man was very much out of my league. He was much older than anyone I had ever been with. I had now become a victim again.

This affair went on for a little while, until I got sick of all the drama. I met my husband around this time, and no disrespect to him, I just wasn't thinking straight. If I had been, I would never have gotten involved with him. He just wasn't what I wanted or needed. He was a bit of a wild child himself, living a life with no consequences. Funny enough, my father introduced me to him, and told me straight away, "He is not for you."

It was like I took him under my wing—someone in a worse state than myself, if that was possible. Somewhere in my subconscious mind, I thought I could help this person. I took the role of carer. This was good, I thought, as I could forget my own issues for a while and look at them later.

I buried myself in this role, totally obsessive. Gone was the party girl. A super-straight girl appeared, a total opposite of what I was. I spent a few years with him. He continued to party hard. I convinced him to make another go at riding. I lifted his self-esteem, but mine was still lost. I seem to hide behind his failures and took them on board as mine. They got in the way of me having to deal with shit I just wasn't ready for.

James hated him from the very start. He kept telling me I was a magnet for losers. Interestingly, he was right. With losers, I didn't have to prove myself at all. I would just shrug my shoulders and not really worry about it too much.

James was staying with me for a while at this stage. He was doing a few little roof-tiling jobs, but bouncing had become his main employment. The roof-tiling had become so awful for James. He worked for a couple of our uncles, and they had given him a terrible time over the years, constantly teasing him, tormenting him, and just being total assholes. That is what they were. The long-term effect on James from this constant badgering would come later, at such a huge price.

James had now also gotten involved with gym work. It seemed to help him. He would take his frustrations out on the weights. I remember one time he told me, "One day I am going to be so bad and mean, no one will ever pick on me again." Over many years, those words came true.

It was during his early bouncing years that James met Jimmy in a gym in a small country town. Through him, my brother met people from the two bike clubs in which he got involved. He would train at Jimmy's gym whilst working in the country. James would spend four days a week there, and the rest of the week he spent either with me or at our Mum's. The life James was heading for we were all terrified of. It was one of evil and darkness that we would never understand. We pleaded with him to look elsewhere for the answers he was seeking, but the constant physical and verbal abuse James had been subjected to was taking hold. His troubled early life had led him to this point.

Unfortunately, this would also be the undoing of my brother's life. He told me after his death—oh, yeah, he visited me regularly to tell me things—that he needed a survival kit; he just picked the wrong one. It's like my own experiences. You have to feel pain in order to feel normal … well, *our* type of normal, which we both knew was not right. It's like, all the abuse makes you become the very person you hate.

James had witnessed so much violence and hated it, but it was where he felt most comfortable. My comfort zone was being with men who were truly bad for me. When no one rescued me as a child, I took that role and reversed it so it seemed like I wasn't a victim anymore. In actual fact, I was always a victim, I just never realized it.

The little boy who was lost in all the years of abuse was now taking a stand. The little boy who had suffered all those years of domestic violence and sexual abuse, and who had been bullied his entire childhood, vowed to me that it would never ever happen again. I suppose the role James took seemed to be his best option. He learned to kick-box and street fight. He took steroids to build muscle, and he grew mean. He became an enforcer of pain. He told me many years later that he was ashamed of what he had done to people, but when he hurt other people it was like he was doing it to feel good about himself.

James and I both blamed our parents for many things. We both never understood why Mum stayed as long as she did. We both blamed her for the child abuse, thinking that if she had left him earlier, it would never have happened. We would never have been subjected to all the violence we were put through. We blamed our father for the violence; if he hadn't been that way, we would not have seen it all. We would not have been sent to our auntie and uncle's house, so the child abuse would never have happened.

I realize now, after many years, that it was no one's fault except those people responsible for what happened. James would eventually treat us all badly in some way, as he couldn't get past the anger. He just couldn't let it go. He hated our father like no one else. He damned this man to hell. The hate died with him. The domestic violence and child abuse would forever change our lives. Even today, I still deal with issues regarding these terrible subjects.

At this time, James became involved with his first bikie club. This was his solitude, his bit of peace. Well, that's what he thought.

He was also involved with a girl he had met whilst bouncing. She was great for him. James told people she was the love of his life, but their relationship paid the ultimate price. The call from the bikie club was stronger. James got himself in all sorts of trouble where this girl was concerned. She tried to leave him a couple of times, and he got violent and angry. He didn't bash her, but he broke into her home and held her against her will. James was now using the one thing he hated most: violent control. He had witnessed for years how our father would control our mother, and now James was using that control against a woman he loved.

James was charged with a serious offence. I was always James's bail, so I ended up going into court with him on many occasions. This is where I learned a little about the law, having to listen to so many cases. I remember asking James what the attraction to the bikie club was. He told me they offered him a brotherhood, a family, something that he had never felt. I believe it was an existence that he found more comfortable than people realize.

It was in the very early years of his involvement with this club that the most significant changes were noticed in James. He was more aggressive towards everyone. His outbursts of anger and aggression were getting more and more frequent. This criminal world he was now in was like going home—the wild parties, the drugs, the women, and pretending that they were above the law brought back all the years we witnessed crime in our childhood. James fit in well. He was young and keen, out to prove himself. He became the enforcer—the enforcer of pain.

James found this role easy to take on, as he was an angry young man. Inside of him was a volcano ready to erupt. James's personality was so volatile, it was frightening to all who were close to him. As his anger rose, so did his ego. Money was also a big drawing card for a young man. The bikie world looked fabulous to James. If only he could have seen into the future, I wonder if he would have still have gone down that road.

I realized something during this time. I always wondered why I moved so much. It was my subconscious thinking that with every move, I could somehow leave all the problems of the past behind. I learned over time that this was not the answer, just as when we were children our parents would often move house with hope in their hearts and the wish of some sort of normality on offer. This would never be so.

As my marriage broke down, I started to learn more about myself than ever before. I was in the single life again, but a little more in control of my own destiny. Even though at times my life still got a little messed up, I was learning to deal with it differently.

As my youth flew past and I recalled sleeping with lots of men, I realized that it was just a way to deal with the stress of child abuse. The party scene for me was fun. If I drank too much or went home with a man, I didn't have to worry about bad memories. I was filling that gap with new ones. I'm not sure if they were any better, but they allowed me time. Through these most difficult days, I can only draw strength from my brother and truly believe that he is still with me, not only in memory but also in presence.

*The truth will set you free.*
*—John 8:32*

*There is no greater agony than bearing an untold story inside you.*
*—Maya Angelou*

# PART TWO

## The Bikie Years

# CHAPTER 5

## *Satan's Sons*

*Bikies.* The very word makes people shudder. Some have very little knowledge of what these clubs are all about. It really is only what one reads in the paper or watches on TV that allows people to get some insight.

Bikies live in a world that they think is beyond the law. They believe they are a law only to themselves. I think they are just grown-up bullies—men who wish to act badly and think because they wear a patch, they have the right. So with that in mind, I'll begin to tell you about my brother's life in the two bikie gangs that he was a member of.

To start this subject off, bikies are people who I truly have no respect for. I think personally they are just some of our country's most horrible individuals—maybe not all of them, but the majority of them. James's involvement with these people put him and our family under extreme pressure and sometimes in danger's way. The stress that these people inevitably caused us—both during James's time with both clubs and after he was out—is unforgivable. Well, that's a strange word, *out*. Are you really ever free?

James was a young man when he met some of the bikies. He was working as a bouncer in the pubs of a small country town in our midwest—a mining town full of hard-drinking men, a town where there was money to be made. James started bouncing at seventeen, a bit young for a lad to be working the door, but a young man who was on his way. James was angry with the world. He was looking for brotherhood, mateship, someone who actually gave a shit.

It was through this job that he entered a gym in this town to work out, as that was James's way of dealing with his anger. A young man who owned the gym befriended James. He was a troubled soul, probably more troubled than we really knew at that time.

James was getting introduced to many interesting people from the different clubs based in the city and in some country towns. These clubs have many chapters. The Italians who ran the inner city were also a bunch of interesting people.

Sam Cunningham was a name that made some people shiver, a tough man not to be messed with. He controlled most of the nightclubs. As a young man, Sam had boxed and earned his golden gloves. He had gotten himself in trouble as a young man and did jail time for drugs. James always told me, "Just because someone doesn't wear a patch doesn't mean they are not involved." The clubs just use these people in other ways.

The criminal world runs deep. It is in every corner we turn. It involves people in high places, and it all revolves around money, power, and control. James found himself attractive to two clubs. They both had men James found interesting. James always seemed to look up to people who had very few morals. I'm sure that in some part of this world, there are bikies who aren't as ruthless, people who don't hold others' beliefs below theirs. But I haven't met them.

The two clubs James would later become involved with were the Satan's Sons and the Devil's Dogs. These people intimidate and manipulate the weak and the weak-minded. My belief is that they can only intimidate you if you let them. Sure, they are frightening to most people; I guess they really never bothered me. As young children, we associated with people who were real gangsters, so these gangs just didn't do it for me. To me, they were pretenders.

Until my brother's untimely death, he associated with people from all walks of life. James was comfortable in the criminal world; it was like going home. He felt a sense of belonging. You could be angry and aggressive and not be told you couldn't be. It seemed the angrier James got, the more respect he earned from his fellow club men. But James's involvement with his first club, Satan's Sons, was a roller-coaster ride from hell.

James was living at my home and Mum's, but he was rarely with either one of us. He would travel to the small country town on Thursday morning and be back home on Monday afternoon. The whole time in between, he bounced at the pubs and nightclubs. He would tell us many stories of the bashings that he would do. The drug scene was massive. Women were plentiful, and you could do as you pleased.

He would stay at the pubs, as they had accommodations for the guys. He spent his days at the gym. He loved doing weights. Doing weights helped relieve the stress that was constantly with him, a tightening across the shoulders and a throbbing in the neck. You just don't ever let your guard down. The fight mode keeps you alive.

He was now learning kick-boxing. The young man who had befriended James was a champion kick-boxer. He had represented Australia. I was told his kick-boxing gym was called Tony's Academy, and James would often attend it. The friendship that started now between James and Tony would follow them through twenty years, though it was often tested, as Tony had bipolar disorder and was hospitalized many times. James would always find excuses for Tony's bad behaviour.

James would often visit Tony whilst he was in hospital. James showed real concern when Tony told him that he had shock treatments for his mental condition. James told us that Tony would lapse into a make-believe world and even fancy himself a mercenary. He thought at one time he was untouchable, even when all hell broke loose. James stood staunchly by him. James was the type of man who, if you were his friend, you would always be his friend. He stood by all the people he had ever cared about.

The world of the bikies to James brought dreams of drugs, money, and doing whatever he wanted. That kept drawing my brother in. A brotherhood, he would tell us. *Yeah, right*, we would think. The very thought of these people make me feel a different kind of anger. I just could understand why grown men wanted to flaunt their lawless ways in other people's faces. They preyed on weak young men who were vulnerable. They led them into a false family unit. If there was ever a message I could give young men, it would be to think really hard about what they want from you. They are not what they appear. They are chameleons. They wait and wait. They suck you in, and by the time you are a prospective member, your life will never be the same

James bought a motorbike, his first Harley. It was a dream come true for him. He had always loved bikes, as he had been riding them since he was three. The joy in his face was so obvious; he was just so proud that he was able to have this magnificent machine. It was red at the time James purchased it. He would later change the colour of his bike to black. He spent so much money on that Harley it was mind-blowing. Not bad for a boy who left school in year 9.

The allure of the bikies drew James constantly. He was like a bee to honey. He had finally found a place he felt like he belonged—a home. So after a small amount of time, he chose one club over another. It was like going for a job interview, working out what one club could offer compared to the other. He eventually joined the Satan's Sons.

He became a prospective member after a short period of time. They sort of let you in and just keep an eye on you. Then, if they think you can serve them, they make you a prospective member. To become a full patch member, you have to do some very nasty stuff. The Devil's Dogs had also wanted James to join them. He made his choice based on the fact that he knew more people at the Satan's Sons than the Devil's Dogs. So he thought joining that gang was the right thing to do.

Prospective members basically do all the shit work; they have to sell drugs, bash people on request, and do other meaningless chores that they are given. James rose through the ranks quite quickly, as he sold many drugs and did many bashings. He was fitting in too well. It was a very comfortable place.

James told us many stories about life in the club. Some stand out more than others. So as I write about specific events, they are the ones that stood out the most.

He told us about an episode when he was sent out with a couple of patch members to pick up a man who owed the club money for drugs. This was a huge test for James. They arrived at the man's house and beat on the door. When the man opened up, they grabbed him, punching him in the face as they were dragging him across the lawn. They pushed him into the car. One of the members sat in the back with him. There was no escape. The member in the back kept punching the man in the body and elbowing him in the face. They drove to the back of the airport, as there was and still is a huge amount of bush there. The planes overhead blocked all noise. The man could scream as much as he wanted. No one would hear.

After James and the other two had bashed this guy to within an inch of his life, they gave the man a shovel and insisted that he dig his own grave. Whilst the man was digging, they were taunting him, telling him he was going to die and no one would ever find him. The man was in total fear for his life, as one of the other members had a gun pointed at him whilst he was digging his grave—pointing the gun and just clicking it onto an empty barrel. This proved to be very useful in handling some people.

Luckily for this man, it would end with a terrible bashing. After he had finished digging the hole, they pushed him to the ground, bashing him over and over again. They decided to throw dirt on him, telling him all the time that they were going to shoot him. He kept pleading for his life, begging for mercy. They just made a joke of it. He was told he had to get the money to the club the next day, or he would be lying down in this hole the next night. The man assured them that if they let him go, the money would be there.

They left the man at the back of the airport covered in blood, bashed beyond recognition. The man did come up with the money the very next day. Lucky for him. I wonder if he ever got himself involved with those people again.

The bikies would sell any kind of drug to whomever. They really didn't care about the people or the families, or the fact that drugs can tear families apart. It all comes down to the almighty dollar. It was like a smorgasbord—whatever you wanted was available. James's eyes would swell up like saucers whenever he talked about the drugs. He could not believe how much money was made by the sale of drugs. It was mind-blowing; the sky seemed to be the limit to the money and the power that came with it.

James's use of steroids in the early days would help him at the gym to build muscle. Steroids enhance your performance and make you able to lift incredible weights. The availability of this banned substance was quite frightening; you just needed to know the right sort of people. It seemed no thought of being fined or even jailed deterred people from selling this drug.

Steroids made James very aggressive and short-tempered. Mum had so many fights with James's doctor, as she was sure he was supplying James with the drug. Mum even went so far as to threaten the doctor with legal action. She threatened to write a letter to the medical board. James knew that Mum was onto the doctor, so another source had to be found.

James got friendly with a couple of horse trainers I had introduced him to, and they would get the steroids for James. He could sell the steroids to the bikies and people at the gym. It was a nice little money-earner. Horse trainers in those days could easily gain access to banned steroids, as most trainers used them on their horses. Supply to James continued on and on; everyone was making money out of it. James was becoming more and more aggressive and out of control, and most times it was scary to be around him. The steroids made him fly off the handle at the slightest provocation. The aggression seemed to be simmering all the time, like a volcano waiting to explode.

The one thing that amazed many people was that James never drank alcohol or smoked cigarettes. He had always told us that he would never be like his father. James never gambled, never filled out a tab ticket. He had only ever been to a casino a couple of times, and then all he did was wander around. In the very early days of James's involvement with the bikies, they thought he was an undercover police officer. They found it really strange that a man of his stature didn't drink.

Another strange thing James did: when they went on club runs, James would not sleep on the ground in the dirt and vomit. He would go off and book himself into a motel or pub for the night. He really did not fit into this world he so longed to be part off. The other members would make fun of James, but he did not give a fuck. James's club name at the bikies clubs was Big Jim.

I asked him once, "Why don't you camp out with the rest of them?"

He replied, "Fuck that, I'm not lying on the ground like a dog."

James's involvement with the bikies was our family's worst nightmare. But James saw a road that looked very familiar to him, a road that had been running through our lives for a long time, a road filled with anger, aggression, and control of the weak. We had watched it all our lives. There were no boundaries to contain anyone, no law to answer to except the code of the bikies, the law of the jungle. It was easy for James because it involved everything we had been brought up with.

James's involvement with the criminal world now extended to meeting more and more people who were involved in crime. The criminal world was only a small percentage of people. They lived in a world outside normal, a world that very few people ever got an inside look at. Being an arsehole to other people was applauded. There was easy money, and you were allowed to be violent. It was expected and condoned.

The steroids were making James bigger and meaner. He told me once that he would become so big and mean that no one would ever fuck with him again. I'm sure this statement was the result of our childhood. He would never allow anyone to hurt him again—well, at least not man to man. My brother was a very strong man physically. His arms were so powerful I saw him once nearly break a man's neck with one arm.

For the better part of twenty-five years, he trained nearly every day with the use of steroids. The drugs made it easier to power-lift weights. They made him feel like he was invincible. They made him truly believe that nothing was ever going to hurt him again. I think that the drug doesn't just mess with your body, it somehow interferes with your mind. The constant use of steroids and a mixture of all the other drugs James was now experimenting with made his very aggressive behaviour a concern for our family.

No matter how much we tried to talk to him about the drug use and what it was doing to him, he just wouldn't listen. He was now so absorbed in the bikies' world it did not really matter what we thought. It was like he had swapped his blood family for the family world of bikies.

His angry outbursts were triggered a lot more quickly than usually. He had a very short fuse. The smallest thing would set him off, and once he started, there was just no stopping him. It was just "get the fuck out of the way." Even if you had a valid argument, it really wasn't worth having the discussion with him. There was just no reasoning.

Sometimes we would hear him pull up and just hope that nothing would be said to start him off. I use to tease James about the bikies clubs and say to him, "The name says it all." That's what they are. He would defend them like a lion defending her cubs. It was with such aggression and intensity that he did this. James would often say to me I should watch what I say, but I made no secret that I truly disliked these people. I would not be intimidated by people I regarded as inferior to me. I believed they took a young man's life and made him into a living nightmare.

For someone looking for leadership, the bikies were a strong force, and they moulded James into what they wanted. They allowed him to be angry—the angrier the better, and he was a young man with a huge chip on his shoulder. There were no excuses necessary; they encouraged him to be mean and they loved it when he hurt people or intimated them. He was becoming their enforcer, and he and his mate Agro were becoming a force to be reckoned with.

James was now bouncing more and more, so it had become easy for him to do things that the Satan's Sons required of him. In these early days, James was bouncing in the city for a company called Priceless Security—the same company he worked for in the small mining town. James would pride himself on how he and another couple of bouncers were cleaning up the streets of the inner city. A newspaper article dated from 1988 tells of the pride James had in himself for helping to get young people off the street.

A businessman called Mr. Sands spearheaded the idea. He would say, "How can you run a safe business when you have kids sniffing glue, shooting up speed, and leaving blood-filled syringes on the ground?" As Priceless Security walked around the streets, the paper stated, "The laneways are empty and the constant patrols by security guard James Jobson ensured there was no loitering or trouble." But now James himself was the trouble he once tried so hard to remove from the inner city.

James was living with a couple of mates in a small house. It was whilst he was working at the local hotel that he met and started dating an Irish girl. She had been married and had two young sons. James would spend a small amount of time with her, but she was a really nice person. She was a slender woman with very short hair and had this amazing accent. But they were really worlds apart.

Their relationship was doomed, and it ended badly. James was doing the wrong thing, and this strong woman couldn't take it anymore. He tried to intimidate her, but she would not put up with his shit. She had James charged, and he became increasingly furious at the situation. He actually got charged a second time for trying to intimidate a witness. He had followed the woman to the local shopping centre and was harassing her. She attempted to drive off, and James smashed her car window. Finally, after months, the case was heard. James was fined, and then he moved on.

He had a young lawyer who represented him over many years named Richard. He is now a district-court judge. But before Richard made the move to the bench, he knew my brother very well. They got on famously, at least until Richard tried to give James some very sound advice. Richard was a handsome slender young man who was always destined for great things. In those days he drove a sports car and was often seen with beautiful young woman. He was always a gentleman; he had a quiet way about him. His father, Jack, also was one of James's legal advisors in the very early days of his criminal run. Patric was a frail old man—I never really remember him being anything else—but still a gentleman in every way.

James had learned from our father that intimidating woman and a strong hand is what was needed. After all the years James had hated our father, he was now becoming very much like him. This was a sad time for our family. The man who James hated most was now starting to look back at him in the mirror. The motto was, "If you beat someone long enough, they will eventually do what you want."

James was getting restless. He just couldn't find a woman who would put up with the life he had chosen. Yeah, sure, there were always the groupies who hung around, but James wanted something more. I thought, *Hmm, here's an opportunity. If I can match James up with someone, this could be just what we need to get my brother back.*

I introduced James to a girl I knew. I had met her through her family, as her father was a horse trainer and sold used cars. They were nice people. I thought she would be good for him. Natalie was a tough girl from another part of the country and had a terrible temper; she just got angry really quickly. She was actually quite frightening at first. You really did not want to be on her bad side.

I remember one time when we were living in a small house. Natalie's dad had his small car yard up on the highway. Natalie was living out in the back of the car yard and was working for her dad. She would help out with the horses and help out at the car yard. Most days, the horses would be walked on and around the car park.

Everyone knows everyone in the racing industry; it's really a small place. Natalie was known to most people, and they all seemed scared of her. Natalie had often vented at the jockeys and had thrashed a couple for mouthing off to her. Jockeys are quite small, so Natalie could intimidate them easily. She would often laugh about grabbing them and threatening them.

This particular day, Natalie came screaming though the car park in her Datsun 120Y, brownish in colour. As she got to the middle of the car park, her car backfired and a large bang went off. A horse trainer we called Ken was walking his good racehorse. The horse had won a few races and was worth a bit of money. Most racehorses are a bit jumpy and nervy. The car just kept on backfiring and making a huge amount of noise.

Ken was yelling out, "You stupid black slut, you're a fuckin' idiot." His horse was jumping around, and he nearly lost control of it. As it was rearing up and kicking out its back legs, he just kept on yelling abuse at Natalie. It really wasn't her fault, and it was not deliberate. The car was still backfiring as Natalie left the car park. She sped off in her car, pulling up at her dad's car yard. She drove the car like a mad thing, slamming on the brakes as she screeched into the driveway.

I was sitting there talking to her dad at the time she came storming in, ranting and raving about what Ken had said to her. Natalie was wired. Her dad stood up. He was a very large man, quite tall and carrying extra weight. He had tight curly hair and was a man with a funny sense of humour. He delighted in the fact that Natalie was so aggressive. He knew she could handle herself; that was never a concern. He said to Natalie, "Don't worry about it. He's a fuckin' idiot, love."

But no, Natalie was going to have him. She was exploding. You could practically see the steam coming out of her ears. Her eyes were glazed over like a white pointer shark. Her nostrils flared. She was pumped. Natalie was on a mission. She went out the back and grabbed a tomahawk. Natalie told us she was going down to cut the fuckin' horse's head off and stick it up his arse.

Just as she got back into her car with the tomahawk and sped off down the road, my brother pulled up on his Harley. We were still having a giggle about Natalie and what she was going on about. James said, "What's going on?" We told James what had happened. He just shook his head, and we waited.

Natalie screamed into the car park in her little Datsun 120Y. It backfired again as she got there. Other people were walking there, and the horses just stopped and stared. Ken was still walking his horse. She pulled up next to him and he again called her a fuckin' black slut. "Look what you're doing! You're upsetting the horse." The horse trainer really had no idea what was about to happen.

Natalie jumped out of the car. The horse trainer was just looking at her. She reached in and grabbed the tomahawk from the back of the car. Natalie started to raise it above her head, saying to him, "Call me a fuckin' black slut, will ya?"

He then realized she was serious. Natalie started to take swings at the horse trainer. His horse was getting more and more stirred up. He was screaming at her to stop it and trying to get away, telling her she was fuckin' mad. Natalie followed on foot, waving the tomahawk, screeching at him that she was going to cut his fuckin' horse's head off and use it as a suppository and shove it up his arse. The more he tried to explain himself to her, the angrier she got, chasing him around the whole car park.

The horse trainer was now as white as a sheet, crying, pleading with Natalie to stop. Onlookers couldn't believe what they were seeing. No one interfered; they just kept their distance. She kept it up, screeching back, waving the axe at his face, telling him he was a fuckhead.

After a period of time had passed, my brother decided to drive down to the car park where they were. Natalie was still pumped and chasing the horse trainer. James pulled up and grabbed the axe from her and said, "Enough. Fuckin' enough."

Natalie was still screaming at the horse trainer She was screeching that she was going to cut him and his horse up into little pieces and feed him to the dogs. The horse trainer pleaded with James to help him. James laughed and said, "Sorry mate, you brought all of this on yourself."

He got her to settle down, and she agreed to go back to the car yard. Natalie's car was still backfiring, so she decided to do a couple of laps around Ken and his horse, still screaming at him. Finally she drove out of the car park. Natalie told her dad that she was still going to get Ken for calling her a black slut. "I'm going chop him up."

Natalie's dad said, "James, take her out for a while. Get her to cool off somewhere."

Natalie was still going on and on about the horse trainer. They jumped on James's Harley and James headed down the road, straight towards the car park, revving his Harley as they drove through. Natalie said to James, "Come on, babe, let's see if he says anything to you."

James just laughed and said, "Not likely."

But the horse trainer had gone. Later he came up to the car yard as white as a ghost, crying at what Natalie had threatened to do. Natalie's dad just laughed at the horse trainer and said, "Ahh, don't worry, she will calm down eventually."

The horse trainer kept on apologizing for what he had said. "I did not realize it was your daughter in the car," the trainer said, going on about the car backfiring and how it was upsetting his horse. It was like something straight out of Monty Python. As serious as it was, it was just a bit funny. Natalie's dad offered the man a beer to calm his nerves. The poor man could not stop shaking. Every time he heard a car pull up, he shit, thinking it was Natalie back again. Natalie's dad just kept telling him to calm down.

At the very same time that James got involved with Natalie, he met up with another woman who we had gone to school with. Jenny was her name. She was a year younger than me, a slender woman with long black hair. Jenny had tattoos on her arms and a huge tattoo on her back. She was no shrinking violet either, and she had a mouth on her. It seemed James had met two women very much the same. If it hadn't rained, it would eventually pour.

Jenny had two small children by a guy who lived not far from us as kids. His brother had been a friend of James's since childhood. He was sent to jail and died in prison not long after that. He had a massive drug problem. James really did not have any time for him at all.

James had gone from no woman to two very tough women who would never meet. James lived this lie so well. I'm not sure what would have happened if these two had realized what was going on. James stayed with Jenny for twelve years. Jenny stuck with him through thick and thin; there was nothing she would not do for my brother. Jenny had come from a split family as well and was an only child.

Natalie's family had a history all its own They were from a known drug-growing capital and were involved with the drug scene over there.

That's what we had been told, that her family was involved with the Italian Mafia. Natalie's family was half Spanish, so she was a beautiful girl with striking looks: clear dark skin and long wavy dark hair. I'm sure the temper she had was from the Spanish blood, as they are well known to be fiery. One of her uncles did a prison term for drugs, and another was a member of the infamous Wild Bears bikie gang in another part of the country. Natalie told us he was very high up in the club. James met him a couple of times, but I don't think they got on.

It seemed wherever James looked or whoever he associated with, he would always be surrounded by some sort of criminal activity. Being brought up in a house where the law was never respected, I sometimes wonder what hope did he really have?

It was in the early years that James's friendship with a few of the club's older members grew. Cain Walsh, who was called Agro, became one of James's closest friends. He was another man with massive problems. He was scary to look at, a tall slender man with dark hair, scars on his face, and tattoos all up his arms. Not much really to look at; I mean, if you passed him in the street, you really wouldn't be bothered about him. James and Agro seem to thrive in their role in the club. It allowed them to bash people for very little reason. They just loved the notoriety that came with the sheer brutality of their role.

James used his brute force, but Agro would always carry weapons. His favourites were his knives. He used to carry them under his jacket. He would often wear a long black trench coat, and when he opened it, inside would be an array of knives. He used to joke and call it his toolbox. Agro had been shot many years earlier and walked with a limp. James really never extended any more information about what had happen to Agro, so we never asked.

The two of them would often go to the person's house that they were going to bash and force their way in with no regard for who was in the house. Whilst the bashing itself would be brutal, they would find joy in hurting people. They would often make the victim clean up the mess whilst bleeding and in pain, something I know James regretted later on in life. He was not proud of it.

We would eventually call Agro "Uncle" after James's eldest child was born. James didn't think it was right that his young son call this man Agro, so Uncle is what we would call him in front of the kids. James use to tell me about their outings and laugh at Agro's antics. They would be driving along the road in the car and Agro would tell James, "I'm bored. Let's make someone shit." So out came the gun, and he would take potshots at things like sign posts, or when cars pulled up alongside them he would point the gun at people just to get a response.

James said it was an adrenaline rush to see people in so much fear. It was the ultimate rush, sometimes better than the drugs that they were on. James was glad of the power in their hands. It was euphoria to these people, but very sad and tragic for the people they bashed. Young girls who would think it cool to be a part of the bikie scene would end up so smashed on alcohol or so drugged out that they would be gangbanged and often have no control over what was happening to them. Some of these girls were fifteen and sixteen, some a little bit older. They never dared go to the police, as fear itself stopped them. They were treated so badly, it was terrible. I cannot imagine why young girls put themselves in so much danger.

James and Natalie decided to live together. Even though Natalie was a tough girl, my brother would wear her out. They constantly argued over James's behaviour and the fact that he never came home. But the money he was earning was massive. The drug world was in full bloom. "There are always suckers," as James would say, "who just have to have drugs." Money was plentiful. They could afford anything they wanted. James and I came from very humble beginnings. We did not have much at all growing up. So James would splurge with his money.

James and Natalie were living in a quiet suburb in a small house not far from the club. When Natalie got pregnant, it shook James for a while, as responsibility was not a word in his vocabulary. A baby was the furthest thing from his mind at that time. Natalie sailed through her pregnancy. James had lost his license at that time, so he relied on other people to drive him around. Jenny was one of those people, with James getting her to meet him up the road. Natalie never suspected anything.

Natalie went in to labour, and as James had no license, Natalie's mum drove her to the hospital. James rang me to pick him up, as he was at the clubhouse. I have never seen so much joy on a person's face as I did that day. When James's baby was born, he was the proudest person on earth. He was holding this precious bundle and tears were in his eyes. He told me he loved this little person from the moment of its birth.

But club life was still calling James. He was given a task to do with three other men. He was still a prospective member at that time. The deal was that he would be nominated to be a full patch member after the bashing. The man they were sent to bash was Steve Justice. He had been a full member of this club, but he owed lots of money for drugs. So it was arranged that James, Agro, and two other men—Jack Dawson and Eddie Whitehouse—would drive down to a country town, Poons Basin, a small wheat-belt place. Steve Justice was living there with his wife, Chris, and daughter, Lily.

The group arrived late at night, got out, went two to the back and two to the front, and so it began. They were masked up with balaclavas and armed with baseball bats. Whitehouse knocked on the door. Lily yelled out, "Who is it?"

Whitehouse yelled back, "It's me, Lily, Eddie. Open up."

Lily went and got her dad. Steve asked, "Is Agro with you?"

Eddie replied, "No."

Steve opened the door, and in they went. Dawson and Whitehouse went in first, punching Steve in the face. James and Agro came from around the back. Whitehouse went into Lily's room. He was grabbing at her and telling her to go with him. The little girl said no. Lily started to scream for her mum to come get her. Dawson was in Justice's wife's room, grabbing her and throwing her in with the little girl. Dawson and Whitehouse tied Justice's wife's hands and gagged her, and then they tied the little girl up as well.

The bashing started. The bikie who had broken club rules was now being dealt with by the law of the jungle. They bashed him senseless. The injures he was left with were multiple compound fractures to both arms, compound fractures to his leg, depressed fractures to both cheeks, broken nose. His wife and daughter could hear the thuds that were being dealt to their husband and father. The whole thing was hideous. James often felt great remorse because of the child being in the house at the time.

Walsh kept yelling at Justice, "You think you can get away with fucking my missus, and then think you can just walk away whilst you owe money?" They recovered the man's patch, as he had now been kicked out of the club. He was told to get the money to the club or he best get his affairs in order, because they would be back, and next time he would be dead. Agro kept going into the room with Justice's wife, pointing the gun at her, saying, "You go to the police, you're fucking dead." It was later stated that Justice's wife heard Agro say a few times, "I should just shoot this cunt now." He had a large pistol in his hand, just waving it around like a madman.

This beating had been ordered by the president of the club himself. The bashing was a success: they had taught Steve a lesson. They all made it through the house and just left them all there. Steve's wife waited until she heard the car go and made it into the kitchen. She found her husband tied up and not moving. There was blood everywhere.

She managed to get a knife and cut herself free, and then she cut her husband free. She saw that the phone had been ripped out of the wall. She later stated that she made her husband as comfortable as possible, took Lily, and went to the neighbours'. The neighbours had been awakened by the sound of a car screeching off, and they went and rang the police. The former bikie went to the police, and even though the men's faces were covered, he told the police who they were. What followed was protocol. The police interviewed the men, and they all had solid alibis. Well, they thought they did.

As time marched on, the police began to break the men and their alibis. James had raced up and had now become a fully patched member of this hideous club. He was so very proud that he got his patch. It meant you were somebody in the club, somebody who now had a voice. The president of the club at this time was a man called Wayne Hunt—not a very nice person at all. James would not hear a bad thing about him or any other member of this club. The more we went on about it, the worse it got.

James had moved to another house, as where they were living had become too hot. James was still very friendly with a couple of the men he had bounced with. They would always just be around selling drugs, making huge amounts of money.

I remember one day being at James and Natalie's when James had gone off down the street. The next minute, the doorbell rang. Natalie opened the door, and there were half a dozen police officers. They had grabbed James down the road and handcuffed him in the street. Natalie refused to open the door and told them to fuck off. They produced a search warrant for the house. James yelled to Natalie to open the front door. Natalie was yelling back at James, "I've got a fuckin' baby in here. These dogs ain't coming into my house." She was screeching.

James said, "Open the fuckin' door before they break it down."

They pushed past Natalie. We were shocked at the sheer arrogance of the police. They made Natalie and me sit in the middle of the floor. Natalie had only a T-shirt on, and she asked if she could get dressed.

"No," they replied. "We told you to sit the fuck down."

One of them went to grab Natalie. She pulled away and said, "Get your fuckin' hands off me."

The baby was only a few months old. Natalie was still mouthing off, as she was not a shy type of woman. She could very well hold her own. She could even intimidate some men.

They searched the house—not very well, I might add. James had a couple of guns hidden in the house, and they simply missed them. James and Natalie had been packing up to move.

The police left the house in a terrible mess. Natalie's younger two siblings were also living with James and Natalie, as Natalie's parents had split up and her mum had taken off and left Natalie's dad with the two youngest. He was not dealing with the split very well, so that is how the kids ended up at James's.

At this time, James and another patch member from the Satan's Sons had decided to open a massage parlour in the inner city. They had rented an old house and fixed it up. They managed to hire a few girls, and James decided that Jenny would run the parlour, as he trusted her. Even though James and Jenny were seeing each other, James made her work in the parlour. Even though it annoyed him, he still made her earn money. The business was going really well.

So with the drug money and now the parlour money, life was good. James had saved enough to put a deposit on a house, but then the police charged James and the other two men with the bashing of Steve Justice. The other two were charged first, so James got Richard to represent Jack

Dawson, as James thought he was in the clear. When James was charged, he had to find another lawyer. For the first time in many years, Richard wasn't his legal representative. James simply did not trust anyone else.

Agro was on the run at that time and wasn't charged. He remained on the run for some time before turning himself in. It was my brother's child's first birthday. We had it at the zoo, and there were a lot of people there. Agro was coming, even though he was wanted. James asked me to go out the front and wait for Agro so I could walk back with him. He finally showed up with his girlfriend, and in we went. We had brought everything with us except a knife to cut the cake. Agro opened up his jacket and said, "Take your pick. They're all clean, no blood, no guts." He was a bit much sometimes.

The party went well, and we all went home. James and the other two were going to defend the case, as they all had alibis. The parlour was booming; business was great. Life could not be any better.

One of the guys James had bounced with and supplied with drugs to sell was named Rolly. They had been friends for many years. At one point, they even shared a house. Rolly was a strongly built guy, very handsome, with dark olive skin. Women just loved him. He had a way about him that was sexy. Unfortunately, he had done the wrong thing, and he owed James a lot of money. He had spent the money that he made from selling drugs and did not pay James what he owed. He decided that James was going to jail and so he didn't have to pay. This went on for a while.

James's theory was that people who had done the wrong thing by him would eventually surface somewhere. James never wasted time looking for them. Like a bad penny, they always turned up. James would somehow always get his man.

While out cruising down the highway one sunny day, on his Harley with the wind at his back and the sun on his face, James was thinking, "Fuck, life is good." Cruising up to a set of lights, James wove through to be at the front. Dressed in his patch and revving the big Harley as he pulled up at the red light, James pulled up next to a car. He looked at the driver and realized it was Rolly. *Hey there, you owe me money, fucker. Thank you, I've been wondering where you were hiding.*

Rolly did not pay much attention at first when James hopped off his motorbike, kicked out the stand, removed his helmet, and left the bike running. James removed his gloves and placed them on the bike with his helmet. He took off his jacket and laid it across the bike. James walked casually over to the car, reached in, grabbed the keys, and said, "You're not going anywhere." Rolly did not see him coming. He never really looked at bikies just in case it was James one day.

James proceeded to bash this man through the opening of the window. The bashing took a few minutes. The lights had changed at least three times, and not one person beeped a horn. People just were amazed at what was taking place in front of them. James pulverized this man until he was satisfied that he had caused and inflicted as much pain as possible. When James was finished, he said to Rolly, "You can run, man, but you cannot hide forever. I am everywhere. I will always find cunts like you."

James turned around and walked back to his bike. Taking his time, he brushed himself off, flicking away little bits of glass. He put on his jacket, gloves, and helmet. Then he simply hopped back on his motorbike, giving the motorists behind him the finger before driving off. True story.

The appearances in court were wearing James down. He was not happy with what was now unfolding, nor were other members of the Satan's Sons. James and the other members had voiced their disapproval to the president and council. They had decided that they would have a challenge for the top job. The other men who stood by James had all been twenty-plus-year members, so they had been there a long time. There was just so much going on at this time. It was chaos.

In the midst of all this were problems with the other clubs about turf for drugs. Unbeknownst to Mum, at some point James and the bikies had buried an arsenal in her backyard. A great deal of money was also hidden. Mum came home one day to a backyard full of bearded men with shovels. They had made a terrible mess, digging up half the yard, but they were having no luck finding what they were looking for. Mum went crazy, but James just told her to fuck off. She still stood there and argued for a while.

"Get in the fuckin' house and mind your own business," he said.

Mum said back, "This is my house, you know."

James just shrugged his shoulders and again told Mum to get into the house. James said that the guns and money had been there for a while. They were standing there discussing what could have happened to all the stuff they had buried. Mum, being stubborn, refused to go inside while they were destroying the yard. She suggested that they go down the road and hire themselves a metal detector. After another couple of hours digging and cursing with still no luck, a decision had to be made. This had gone on nearly all day. Finally they went and hired a metal detector to find the guns.

What had happened was that movement in the ground had shifted the soil. The guns and money were at the back fence going into the neighbours' yard. It became like a treasure hunt. They were all arguing who was going to use the metal detector. Then they finally got what they had come for. The metal detector was going right off with the sound it makes. "Beep beep, you fuckin' beauty!" one of the bearded men yelled out. They could not believe how far the gear had shifted. As they were standing there discussing it, Mum was ordered again into the house. But as is only human nature, Mum peered out the back window. *My goodness*, she thought as large objects were removed from the hole in the ground.

One weapon after another was recovered, and then finally the money, which was in a tin. They took off the covers to the weapons to make sure they were not damaged. There were rifles, handguns, a crossbow, and a rocket launcher. Mum said she just shook her head and thought, *Wow. I wonder what all this is going to be used for? We aren't at war with anyone.* But the bikie war was coming.

They loaded the weapons into the cars that were waiting and removed themselves from Mum's house, leaving her backyard all dug up. Mum was not impressed at all. In fact, she rang James and told him to come back and fix the yard. James just chuckled and said, "Yeah, right."

The problems that had been brewing were now been felt right through the club. The club was a bit divided over the conflict, and the threat of a challenge wasn't going down well with the president. The trial had been set for James and the other two, Jack Dawson and Eddie Whitehouse The problems between the clubs was growing, with bashings all over town My brother's personal life was in chaos, with two women and so many lies to tell to keep each one where he wanted her to be. Jenny had read in the paper that James had a child. James then told her that Natalie was a lesbian friend of his and he was helping her out by donating sperm. It was just insane that they actually believed what he told them.

Jenny was still running the parlour for James. As the men were getting ready for their trials, it was agreed that they would continue to fight the case. All the time, Dawson and Whitehouse were making a deal with DPP behind James's back. He was being railroaded by these men who he thought were staunch and true club men. Agro was still on the run; there was no luck finding him.

The trial was about to begin. All three were in custody and waiting in the dock at the back of the courtroom. There were about twenty members waiting to see what was going to happen. I was sitting in the front when Richard approached me and asked if he could have a word. James looked puzzled; he still had no idea that the other two had made a deal. Richard wasn't James's lawyer, but he knew our family well. He told me that the others had made the deal to plead to lesser charges. The judge was in favour of this as it saved the little girl and her mother having to take the stand. The DPP had worked out what charges they were to plead guilty to.

An agreement was made. James's lawyer went out to talk to James. My brother was so furious. He had just been shafted. He was arguing with his lawyer, screaming at him, telling him that he had sold him out, and he was fuckin' useless. He told his lawyer to fuck off and get away from him. I went to talk to James, and he was a broken man. I talked to him about what was going to happen, and then Richard came over and James listened to him. He explained to James that there was nothing he could do. James kept asking Richard, "What should I do?" He was in a terrible state. This is not how this was meant to be. "Fuckin' dogs!" he was yelling. "You fucking dogs!"

Richard said to James, "I'm sorry, mate."

They were taken back into the docks. The president said, "How is James?"

I said, "What do you think? Some club you got. You're all dogs."

Turning back around, James was in a daze as Judge Jupp listened to what Mr. Worthington was saying. He described the attack as every household and parent's nightmare. He stated that Mr. Justice had been attacked in a vicious and cowardly way. But because of the club code, the real reason for the attack was never told. The judge set down a date for sentencing. I was gobsmacked. Just as I thought. I knew they were no good. As we got outside, the president approached me again and made some smart comment. I just stared at him, and we started to argue. I told him he was a prick. "You're supposed to be the president, and yet those two just sold out James and Agro."

I was so angry. I had to go home now and tell my mum. She would be devastated. As I was driving home, my mind was abuzz. I knew they were no good. James should not have gotten himself involved with theses jerks.

The sentencing date came around real quick. We went back into court to hear what was going to happen. Judge Jupp didn't mince words. He made it very clear that they would be given long sentences. While he was looking at his paperwork, I thought, *Well, since all four were involved, they would surely all get the same amount of time.* Boy, how wrong I was.

The judge called Dawson and Whitehouse up first. He gave Dawson two years and sent him to a medium-security prison. *Good*, I thought, *that's were all the dogs and paedophiles go*. Whitehouse was next. He got eighteen months. *Hmm*, I thought, *looking good for James*.

Then he gave James seven years.

James put his hand on the bench. He was shattered. How could those two get such short terms and he got seven years? They were all involved with the whole episode. James was clearly in a mess. He called out to me, and they let me approach him. He grabbed me and told me he loved all of us, and he asked me to help Natalie with the baby. It was so horrible. James held on so tight. He was the little boy lost all over again. People he thought he could trust had fucked him once more.

I rang Mum from the courthouse. Everyone was clearly very emotional and upset. The club president was outside again, and we got into another argument before I walked away. As I was driving home, I was so upset. I was crying so much I could not see the road. I was living in a small leafy suburb at the time not far from the Satan's Sons clubhouse. I got to my driveway, and then I pulled back out again.

I still don't know what possessed me, but I drove to the clubhouse, got out of my car, stormed through the gates, walked past a couple of very large bearded men, opened the door, and walked in. The club president was at the bar with a few more men. I walked over and said, "You fuckin' prick. What sort of tough boy's club is this? Two of your members just rolled on the other two. They sold them out, and you let them do this. You knew.

You are filth. You are all not worthy of calling yourself a brotherhood. You don't even know what it means. You are happy because James and Agro can't challenge you now. You told them to bash Justice. You should be in jail with them."

He just sat there and said nothing. Lucky for me, I guess, because I was a bit outnumbered, and I could have been in all sorts of trouble. I turned and walked out.

The very next day, we were allowed to go and see James. He was at a maximum-security prison. Natalie and I went; Mum was still so distraught, she wasn't really up to it. When we arrived, they searched Natalie and me, and they were very rough. Natalie just mouthed at them, she wasn't holding back. James walked into this large room filled with prisoners and guards and visitors. He was dressed all in green with thongs on. He walked over to Natalie and just hugged her. He grabbed me and gave me a hug too. We all sat down. James was still trying to come to terms with the fact that he got seven years.

He was still very raw. This big bad man was now like a small mouse in this terrible place. I had no worries for his physical safety; James could look after himself. It was the mental part that had us worried. He had informed me that he already knew I had gone to the clubhouse and vented at the bikies. He grabbed my hands and said, "Look, I know you were just doing what you thought was right, but you could have gotten hurt. I can't protect you at the moment."

It was like I knew what he was saying was true, but I had always looked out for James, and this was no different. He made me promise that I would not do that again. I said, "Yep, whatever you want."

He said to me, "You are very lucky they did not hurt you." He then asked Natalie if she had she heard anything. Natalie mentioned that they wanted to keep his bike.

"Why?" said James.

"I don't know," Natalie answered.

James looked puzzled. He had trusted the wrong people again. As tempting as it was to say I told you so, I just could not say it. Looking at my brother feeling so sad, I could not be so mean. We sat there chatting for a while about trivial stuff.

It was a horrible place. I asked James what it was like, and he said, "It's more awful than you can imagine." He had only been there a day. He had heard screams at night, screams that haunted him the whole time he was in prison.

It was time to go. I could see on James's face how much he just wanted to come with us. It was so sad. As we all stood up to leave, James cuddled each of us. I did not want to let him go. He whispered to me, "Tell Jenny to come tomorrow."

"Okay," I said.

Natalie seemed to get harassed quite a bit with the random searches when she was visiting James. They always seemed to want to search her. I never even got touched at any of the visits.

I remember her telling me about an episode. She had taken our young sister with her to visit James. Natalie signed them in, and then the woman screw announced to Natalie that she was to be searched. Natalie started to vent her disapproval. They went to search our young sister when Natalie screamed at them, "Leave her alone, she's only a fuckin' kid, you fuckin' pervs."

They then informed Natalie that she was to be strip-searched.

"What?" Natalie yelled. "You're not fuckin' touching me, you lesbian slut."

The woman screw then pulled out a pair of rubber gloves and flicked them on.

Natalie said, "You're fuckin' sick. You must get enjoyment out of touching other people's private parts."

The woman told Natalie to step into the other room, leaving our young sister with the toddler.

Natalie was pumped again. "You sick fuckers!" she kept yelling. They told Natalie to remove her clothes. As Natalie was taking off her top, she was saying to the woman screw, "Having a good look, are ya?" The woman went over and started searching Natalie, first touching her breasts. Natalie was going crazy. "Having a good feel, you fuckin' lesbian?"

The woman had obviously heard it all before and just continued on. She told Natalie to remove her jeans and underwear. Natalie was still screaming as she removed the bottom part of her clothing. The woman told

Natalie to bend over. Natalie said, "You're sick," but she bent over anyway, opening up her bottom cheeks and yelling, "Having a good look, are ya?" Finally it was over. Natalie got dressed and stormed into the visit. James did not know what was wrong. Natalie was screaming, telling him what had happened. James tried to calm her down.

The screws walked over and told Natalie if she did not quiet down, she would have to leave. She spat at them. The prison guard told her to get up and get out. He went to grab her arm, and she hissed at him, "Don't touch me, you fuckin' dog." James just shook his head. There was nothing he could say or do.

Over the next few weeks, things got real interesting. The Satan's Sons had sent a couple of men around harassing Natalie for money for protection. She told them to fuck off. The club president had now told another long-term patch member, White, to go and tell James that they were kicking him out of the club. White asked why. The president said, "Because he is no good to me in jail." But the real reason was that James and Agro had made the challenge for leadership of the club before the trial, and now the president was free to do what he wished.

White had been a member of this club for more than twenty years. He was so disgusted he argued with the president over the decision. He even called a meeting of the whole club to try to get the decision overturned, explaining to the members that it was the wrong thing to do. James had earned his place in the club and was entitled to stay a member until he got out and had a chance to be heard. But the president convinced the other members that he had the right to kick James out, as he was the president. He asked other members if they'd like to challenge him. No one replied.

White eventually got out, and down the road he joined the Riddlers club. He was made full patch member right away and made second in charge. The Riddlers were new to our state at this time and were on the lookout for members.

White was a good friend to James. He visited James quite often whilst James was in jail. He used to tell James about the Satan's Sons president and what he had been up to. He told James that he was joining another club and that James should too.

James had a terrible time in prison. It wasn't just the fact that he was locked up, but also what went on in there. James was so angry at some of the other prisoners. On the outside, they were ruthless criminals and not very nice people at all. In jail, some of these men raped young men who were sent in. Some of these young guys were only eighteen or nineteen and had traffic offences. They should have been sent to minimum-security, where they might have had more of a chance. James told us that sometimes he could hear the young men scream in pain, and they would be crying. James told us the term in jail is that these young men got soured.

The cries were haunting, James would tell us when we went for our visits. He said it was so traumatic.

I asked, "Why don't you go help them?"

He answered, "I am just one man. The screws don't give a fuck about what is going on." He said a couple of these young guys approached him and asked if they could share his cell for protection. James just did not want to get involved. The prisoners who were raping these young men made it quite clear to James that he should stay out of it, as it wasn't his business. They told him that if he chose to get involved, he would be sorry. James said to them, "I don't give a fuck about you" and warned that if they came near him, he would kill them. He told them to fuck off, stay away from him, and not to bother speaking to him again. They kept their distance. James was so angry that these young men were being treated like pieces of meat.

James wouldn't let anybody share his room at that stage; he would just tell them that they were going to be okay and to keep themselves around other people. James was trying to encourage them to stay strong, even though he knew what was happening to them. James was doing his time there. Very tough gang rapes and bashings unfortunately became a way of life for some of these unfortunate young men. James told me he would awaken from nightmares, but he would not tell me about them. I wonder sometimes if the young men being raped awakened James's memories of a past he really did not want to revisit.

Whilst this was going on, I started to see a man who also had criminal convictions, mainly for drugs. James had not met him before he went to prison, and we were now living together. I had been working at our local pub, and I had met him there years before. He had been remanded to a low-security prison for about eighteen months for charges related to a boatload of marijuana that had come in on the coast of a small fishing village. The boat was estimated to be carrying about thirty tons.

His involvement was later dismissed by a jury. A few of the other men who had been charged pleaded guilty and were given lengthy jail terms. Carl and a few others fought and won in the district court.

The shipment was split; some of it went to the east coast and the rest went to the city. They lost a truckload, and it was rumoured to have been hijacked by the Devil's Dogs bikie gang. The story went that they knew about the shipment, and when the driver of the truck fled in a panic, they took what was in the truck, and superbly. That's how their clubhouse was built, so the rumour goes. Well, you know rumours—what could be true probably is.

Well, back to jail. A man I had known at the pub where I worked was now also up on drug charges. His name was Brent. He was another Kiwi who I had come across many years before. He was based on the east coast for a very long time. I was told that he was also a part of the Mr. Amsterdam syndicate that was run by fellow Kiwi Troy Cane. When things got hot on the east coast, Brent came to the west to make his fortune in the drug business. He was a real likable rogue and always had a story to tell. He warned me about Carl, the man I was living with. He had told me repeatedly that Carl was no good.

I used to say, "I thought all you Kiwis stuck together."

He would answer, "Only the good ones," and we would just leave it.

On Sunday nights, we would often go down to a local restaurant and have a meal. There was always a group of men who Brent was friends with, and I would often ask a couple of girls who I worked with to join us. These were real criminals; they didn't need a patch on their backs to be somebody. They were the silent ones, the ones people should be more worried about.

Anyway, Brent was headed for jail, and even though he was old and tough, jail scared the bejesus out of him. He knew my brother was in prison and asked me to go see James and see if Brent could share a cell with him for protection. He would make it worth his while. Brent got sent to jail, and we had arranged through James to have Brent share his cell. James had never met Brent before, and I knew that whilst he was sharing a cell with Brent, he would at least have a laugh.

James found it hard at first, as he was wary of everyone, especially with what he had seen going on in prison. It wasn't long, though, before James and Brent got on quite well. Brent referred to James as "the muppet" because James had this insane haircut, but he took it all on the chin.

James had been in prison for about six months when Christmas came around. I had organized Christmas to be at my new home, so everyone was there. James and Brent rang, and we all had a bit of a laugh. James was still finding the restrictions of jail hard. He missed his child so very much.

By now, more dramas had started with the Satan's Sons. They had James's bike and wouldn't give it back. We went and had terrible arguments with the president, but as usual, he was just smug. Gosh, that man pissed me off so much, I just wanted to smash him in the face. We finally got the money they required for us to get James's bike. It was paid over, and the bike was released. I was so glad to see the back of them. They truly were dogs.

James felt trapped being in prison. There was nothing he could do but wait it out. He was spending as much time at the prison gym as was allowed. The good part of this was that he was off steroids and any other drug he had put into his system. You could see a real change in him for the better. He promised us all that the bikies were no more, and he would go straight on his release. The sad thing is, we all believed him. So we were encouraging him to look for different businesses that he could do himself.

Finally he was moved to a farm. It was a minimum-security prison about an hour's drive away. James could have visits on Saturday and Sunday, so he had Jenny visit him one day and Natalie the other. They never collided, but it was getting increasingly difficult to keep up the charade. Jenny was getting suspicious, but somehow he pulled it off.

White continued to visit James and inform him about what was going on at their old club. James told White that he was out and not really interested, but he listened anyway. Brent had been released, and we heard many a stories from him about his holiday in prison. He told me James was doing it really hard, but we knew this anyway.

The time at the prison farm was going along smoothly … well, at least we thought it was. James was in his room one day when all of a sudden he was set upon by six men. They took him by surprise and gave him a thrashing. After the beating, they left the room. James being James picked himself up, went off to the shower block, and cleaned himself up. He was covered in blood but would not give them the pleasure of seeing him like that. He then went to the screws and told them he needed to go to the hospital, as he had a broken jaw. They laughed at him and said, "How?"

He replied, "It does not matter, but I need medical attention."

One of the screws looked at his jaw and realized that he was telling the truth

James was taken to hospital. He was admitted and had a police guard so that he could not escape. We were rang by Natalie, who had been called by the prison officer. We went to the hospital. James had been operated on by that time and was high on morphine. Loving the morphine, he was zapped right out. He was hallucinating and talking rubbish. It was the first time in about a year that James experienced any type of freedom, even though he was chained to the bed.

He explained to us what had happened. He was convinced that the Satan's Sons president had put these men up to the bashing.

I said, "Do you know who they are?"

He replied, "Yeah, what do you think?"

Knowing my brother, I knew that he would wait and get them one by one when the time was right.

He said, "That fuckin' Satan's Sons president, weak cunt, couldn't come and do it himself. Fuckin' dog, he will get his someday."

James was thinking about the future more and more whilst he was laying in that hospital bed. He was there for a few days, and then he was sent back. He now had what they call a "glass jaw." But he would heal, and time marched on.

A couple of his mates from the Devil's Dogs went to see him a couple of times. James had voiced anger at choosing to join the wrong club, but that's life, and it goes on. The men who had bashed my brother were very wary of him now, as they knew he would retaliate sometime. And although it didn't happen until years later, he eventually did. He found each and every one of those six men who jumped him. He bashed each one individually and got even with them all. He told them he would get them, and he did just that. With everyone he bashed, he bashed them a little harder to remind them of how it took six of them to bash him.

James was allowed home on weekend visits, and we would all go to his house just so he could spend time with everyone. Natalie would put on a spread, but she was always agitated. Whilst James had been in prison, she'd had as much freedom as she wanted. Now with James coming home, her wings would be clipped. Whilst standing in the kitchen, James and Natalie got into a terrible argument. She pulled a huge knife out of the drawer, held it to James's throat, and said, "I will kill you. I will cut your fuckin' throat." James just pushed her hand away and told her to fuck off.

During this time, Agro had handed himself in and was awaiting sentencing. The other two had gotten out earlier, as they were serving less time than James. Agro got seven years too; he and James were the ones who got screwed over. He did his jail time easy, as he had been to prison before. He really did not care.

Finally the day came when James was released. He had a couple of years of parole left, but he was just so happy to be out. He had made some friends whilst in prison. They become associates of his on the outside. James had only been home a couple of days when the Devil's Dogs came calling again. They wanted him to come join them, and this was apparent by what they said to him and what they offered him.

*Keep your friends close, but keep your enemies closer.*

# CHAPTER 6

## *Devil's Dogs*

Well, staying away from the bikies did not last long. White had asked if James wanted to come with him to the Riddlers, but the Devil's Dogs sang a sweeter song. They offered James a full patch within six months. He did not have to be a prospective member, he would slip straight in. He would accompany Milo Calabrese on missions. We'd all known it wouldn't be long before James was drawn back to that side of life. We just thought it would be later rather than sooner.

James did not really like Frank, the club president at the time and also the club face. James just thought of him as a rapist who got lucky. Their hatred and hostility towards each other would eventually be a turning point for James. But Frank had been a long-time member and had been around in the Blues days. Blues rock was run from 1986 to 1995. The event itself attractive thousands of people. The police would ensure things went as well as possible. They'd send undercover police in to collect intelligence on known criminals. The Devil's Dogs made huge profits from the running of Blues. Eventually, it was closed down.

I only ever went once to Blues. I felt very uncomfortable there. Drugs were plentiful, and women and men behaving very badly just was not my scene. James had taken me there, so unfortunately I could not leave. The only good part of the whole Blues thing was the music. But my opinion is just that—it's mine. Many people who were not connected to the bikie world loved it.

As James was slowly getting his life back, he applied for a new gun license. He had asked Mum to go with him; I'm really not sure why. But because of his time in prison and the seriousness of it, his gun license had been revoked. James still loved to go shooting with our family, as most of them held gun licenses for kangaroo shooting. So James and Mum went to the police station.

James filled out all the paperwork. Mum was just sitting there. Other people were at the police station waiting. The police officer was reading information on the computer when all of a sudden the printer started to push out paper after paper of James's criminal record. The police officer look bewildered. He made a comment to Mum that "he can't be serious, there is no way in hell he will get his gun license back."

Mum was just sitting there watching the printer. The other people in the station heard the police officer's comment.

James had now gotten off the phone, and he walked up to the police officer. "Well, how about it? You going to reinstate my license or what?"

"No way," the police officer said. "Are you on some form of medication or what?"

James just laughed. "Why, what's the problem?"

"All of this, mate, what do you think?"

James shrugged his shoulders and said, "Man, you don't get it. I don't need a bit of paper to get a gun. I just would like to go shooting with my family."

The cop said, "Can't help you, mate."

"Ahh, fuck it," James yelled and walked out. "Come on, old girl, this is just a waste of fuckin' time. Dogs!" James yelled as he walked out. "Oh well, fuck it, I'll just go shooting anyway."

James still had the two women on the go as well. Jenny would do whatever he asked her to do. Natalie was a bit restless whilst James was in prison. She found a sense of freedom when she did not have to answer to him. She could just run and run all she wanted. James's release clipped her wings. James had gone back on his promise to everyone, but he convinced her he would be doing it for the money and that was all.

White, who had become part of the new Riddlers chapter in town, had been out one night and arrived home to a shower of bullets. They had waited for him to enter his house and fired the bullets across the front of his house. They had obviously been waiting for him. This was a warning from the Satan's Sons about him going off and joining another club.

On this I have to make a comment. My brother was the only one ever referred to as a turncoat or dog by the newspapers in this state, while Milo and others have never been called those terrible names—yet they did exactly what he did. Milo was even worse, as he was the sergeant in arms at the Devil's Dogs. A bit one-eyed by the local media and newspapers. James never liked talking to the media, whilst Milo loved the notoriety. I think Milo enjoyed reading about himself in the papers.

White had bigger problems coming. He would be charged later with serious drug offences and end up in jail for a period of time himself. The Riddlers were not impressed by the Satan's Sons low antics. There was real concern, as the Riddlers wanted payback. It would come.

Meanwhile, word had got out that James had joined the Devil's Dogs. The Satan's Sons president was trying desperately to hold on to his position as president of his club. He was out to prove that he was still the boss and the big man he believed he was. The power was slowing slipping from his grasp.

What could he do? What terrible thing had he authorized? This is a guilt he alone has to live with, but to feel something you really do have to be human first. Guilt really only ever comes to people who have a conscience, something I think the Satan's Sons president does not have. He is a mean man with terrible secrets.

James loved smoking marijuana. He would pull bucket cones one two three. James just loved it. He would ring me up whilst he was pulling a cone, coughing his guts out. I would ask if was okay and hear, "*Cough cough splutter*. Yeah, all good."

"What's going on?" I would ask.

"Nothing," he would say. "How is Super Crim doing?" That's what he called the man I was living with.

"Yeah, right." I would just laugh it off.

The Devil's Dogs were loving James. He and Milo together—they were the twins from the apocalypse, both very big and angry men. Even though they were similar in lots of ways, many thing about them were different. Milo loved to do hard drugs and drink, while James did not drink. Womanizing, they both enjoyed.

It was whilst James was at a party at the inner-city clubhouse one New Year's Eve that he met another woman. Like two wasn't enough! Three was obviously better. This woman had some influence around town and was well-known to most criminals in this part of the world. Her name was Maria. She was different from all the women James had ever gone out with—another strong personality, but a woman who knew where she was going. It was instant attraction.

Maria was very well-educated, a tall woman with a medium to large frame, a little plump and slightly attractive in a weird sort of way. She had dark hair and was very well-spoken. Not my brother's usual type, but strangely, women in high-profile jobs are often attracted to men who have a criminal past. Not all women, just some.

Life for James was on a high. He was where he wanted to be—back in the thick of club people. He would rave about the Devil's Dogs, how different they were from the Satan's Sons. They were true brothers and held their code very seriously. I'm not sure why he tried to sell them to us, as we had no time for any of them. It did not matter what patch they had on, we were never going to be convinced that they were any different from the Satan's Sons They still sold drugs, they still bashed and hurt people. I'm not sure how James thought they were any different.

The situation with Maria is that she knew about Natalie. James had at least told her that much. As for Jenny, James played their relationship down, so Maria though that Jenny was just a business partner, a hanger-on. James had told Jenny that Maria was a money ticket and that she would be able to help him if he got himself in any trouble.

Jenny brought the story. James had sold their relationship as purely platonic. James told so many lies to all these women, I'm not sure in the end if he knew what was real and what wasn't.

James and Milo were powering along doing all the dirty deeds that had to be done. James was just loving being at that damn clubhouse He would stay over there for days. He had rekindled some friendships that had faded over the last few years.

The bikie world was happening. James still had other friends outside the club, people of little morals, not good people at all really. There were also some people who he held in high esteem. So James's friends were from the lowest of people to people who were quite influential. Some had been his friend through the Satan's Sons saga and before that. Tony Frankino was one of those people.

James had met Tony in the small mining town where they trained together. Tony helped James compete, but that was a lifetime ago. James's life was taking a different road, one that Tony could not follow him down. Tony had been busy trying to make a reputation for himself. Both clubs really did not think much of him at all; they actually thought he was full of shit. He would rave about things he had supposedly done, but no one really knew if any of it was true. Most off the bikies thought he was full of piss and wind. He blew his own trumpet, but there was no orchestra at the end.

He told James he had spent time in a Thai jail. He had been arrested for smuggling guns and drugs for the Khmer Rouge. I really am not sure about this; it could be he was just trying to big-note himself. No one really ever thought he was capable of much. James would invite him to the Devil's Dogs club to spend time with him. James tried to get some of the other members to spend time with Tony too, but again, they really couldn't cope with him. They nicknamed him the Flipper, because of the fact that Tony had a mental illness. They just believed he was very unstable. Most of them believed he blew smoke up his own arse.

James and Milo were busy doing whatever needed to be done. If anybody owed the club money or had done something that the club was not happy with, James and Milo were sent to deal with them. James and Milo loved the power. They were flying

Frank, the Devil's Dogs president, was drinking at a hotel in another suburb in May 1998, watching skimpy barmaids. It was well known that this hotel was frequented by the Satan's Sons. It was one of their haunts and where they distributed drugs. Frank knew this when he went there, but he liked rubbing salt into the wound. The most amazing thing is, he went alone.

When he got up to leave and walked outside, he was set upon by a group of Satan's Sons bikies. They bashed him and bit off part of his ear.

They gave him a thrashing to remember. They warned him not to drink there and threatened that next time, he wouldn't be so lucky. They warned him this was their part of town, and he had no business being there. But Frank had an arrogance about him—a man of big build, tall heavy-set, and just so full of himself.

Four days later, another Devil's Dogs member was admitted to hospital with gunshot wounds to his leg. This was really the starting point of that bikie war. On interviewing the bikie, the police could not charge anyone. The wall of silence was up, and there was little the police could do but wait to see where the chips fell.

With every attack, the bikie clubs were getting more and more publicity. Some members of both clubs loved the notoriety; others shunned it.

A few weeks later, a Satan's Sons bikie had both his legs broken and was beaten severely by a gang of masked men armed with baseball bats, in what was a carefully planned raid on a local factory, in broad daylight. Bikies truly believe that they are above the law, that they are a law unto themselves. These men bashed their victim to within an inch of his life, wearing masks so they could not be recognized.

I asked my brother once, "Why do people cover their faces? Are they only brave when the person they are attacking cannot look them in the eye? If these men were brave enough to bash someone, wouldn't you want them to know who did it?" I find the way they mask up to be an act of cowardice.

The scale of the war stepped up a notch. When a Devil's Dogs bikie was caught near a Satan's Sons bikie's house, armed with a fully automatic shotgun commonly known as a "street sweeper," the rumour at the time was that the bikie was to be killed as a stern warning to the enemy. There was a picture of this gun on the news, and how terrifying it looked. The weapons that these clubs could get a hold of was frightening.

The police designated a special task force, which was named Operation Giant. But the war kept raging on. Another Satan's Sons member, Martin Day, was dragged out of his van by four men and beaten with clubs and iron bars outside his home. These men were brutal—no caring about who saw them. The beatings were getting more and more violent. They didn't care who saw them because they knew most people would be too scared to testify. They really played the odds. I do understand why people don't do this, but if the majority of people stood up, the bikies are only a small minority.

As the weeks rolled on, it seemed like every day the headlines were on about more bashings. James's house had a huge brick wall around it, but this was not going to keep anyone safe. James had begun to feel uneasy about the way this war was heading.

James was at home one night with Natalie and their young child, and everyone was asleep. James awoke in the early hours of the morning to noises outside. He noticed the house was full of smoke. James screamed at Natalie to grab their child and get out the back. James went out the side to see what the fuck was going on.

Someone had torched his car, and there was petrol everywhere. They had obviously botched up what it was they were sent to do, because even though it was terribly frightening, no one got hurt, and there was minimal damage. James had cars parked in the driveway, and they had a bit of damage.

Natalie was screaming, "What the fuck is going on? You said we would be safe here! Who the fuck did this?"

James was trying to gather his thoughts, which was not working. James rang Milo and Sambo and explained what had happened. Sambo was a senior member of the Devil's Dogs. He had known James from the early bouncing days. He was the one who asked James to join the Devil's Dogs, and he is someone I dislike a great deal.

The boys went to where James was living. There were about twenty of them on bikes, and others came in cars. The police had arrived and the news crews. There were people everywhere The bikies were standing guard out in front of James's house. The police had warned them not to take matters into their own hands, but they were not listening. They would have revenge. They were their own law.

That was the moment James realized that his family was vulnerable. He decided it was time to move again, so he went out and bought another house near the clubhouse. Natalie was now pregnant with their second child. The move to the north side got James closer to the clubhouse and closer to Maria, as she lived on the north side as well. James had this notion that the closer he lived to the clubhouse, the safer his family would be.

James was doing okay. He rented the other house out for a while. He now was riding that wave again. They thought they were invincible. The war between the clubs was simmering. Both clubs were out to prove who was the toughest.

Meanwhile, Agro had gotten out of jail. He was a seriously unwell man. He just wanted to end it all. He'd had enough. He had woman problems and money problems. In the end, he took his own life, which was sad for his family. He had tried many times over the last few years but had botched them up. Agro suffered a mental disorder that in the end took over his life.

James had been looking for a business for a while. He really just wanted something real. I think he was spending more and more time with Maria. She had originally come from interstate, where her old boss was charged for tax evasion and was slugged with a huge bill. In 2000, he was charged alongside Giuseppe Agentino with conspiracy to murder Jason Corndell and his father, Wally Corndell. He was a high-profile person over east with high-profile clients. In 2008, the prosecution dropped all charges against him. Unfortunately, most of the men who were in an Italian gang were all murdered. Agentino was murdered on the eve of his trial. This was a real blow, as the crew was now no more. Their run had come to an abrupt end. Many of these characters appeared in a hit series, and many books have been written about their antics.

James and Milo were selling drugs to a few different people They would meet up at the local hotel and book a room to do their drug transactions. This was making them both quite a bit of money. They were still sent out to deal with people who owed the club money, but in all seriousness, if you saw these two men pull up, you would either find the money or run. They were men you just did not fuck with. They found pleasure in the fact that they could terrorize people.

The brewing war was starting to bubble again, with people getting bashed from both clubs. Threats were being made. The turf for the drugs was being drawn. The clubs had other groups trying to muscle in as well. One was the Swift Boys, a group of men mainly of Lebanese Australian heritage. They had been around since the 1990s and were slowing building their empire. They were noted for selling poor-quality drugs, and the bikies were not happy. Their story is in someone else's book.

The theory was that in the inner city, whoever mans the door controls the drug trade. So many of the bikies frequented the clubs to supply drugs to the doormen. The Italians were always there. They had agreements with the clubs, so the animosity between them was kept to a minimum.

James and Maria had been searching for the right type of business. She was constantly in his ear to get out of the club, but James just said no, he was where he belonged. Eventually James and Milo were caught at the hotel with a few pounds of marijuana. Jenny had just left; she also had drugs on her. She noticed the cops behind her, so she throw the drugs out of the window. But the police had another car behind, and they stopped and picked it up. The police pulled Jenny over. She was in fine form, screaming abuse at the police officers.

All three were taken into custody and taken to police headquarters They were charged with conspiring to supply and sell marijuana. The pressure was now on. The police were determined to make someone talk. But with all the pressure, James never uttered a word.

The time had come for James's second baby to be born. As usual, James was off elsewhere when Natalie went into labour. She rang him screaming that the baby was coming. James rang an ambulance, as he was on the other side of town. Natalie was rushed to the hospital. Whilst she was travelling to the hospital, James was telling her, "Don't push, I'm nearly there. Wait for me."

Natalie was screaming, "Don't push? You cunt, you try stopping a watermelon coming out your arse. I can't stop the baby, you fuckin' idiot."

So James's second child was born on the way. By the time Natalie got to the hospital, James was there. He was so chuffed at having another baby. He loved his children with all that he was. He so wanted to be a good dad, but he'd never had a role model, so it was really hard for him. This would be one of his biggest struggles.

Meanwhile, the police had decided to search our mum's house. They were bumping up the pressure on James, constantly harassing James and Milo. They got a search warrant and went to Mum's. They found nothing, but this was just one of many raids. The harassment continued; poor Mum got raided over and over.

It was about three weeks after Natalie came home from the hospital that James jumped into his old Ford and headed to the clubhouse. It was a cold day, it being July. As he pulled out of their drive, he noticed a car at the other end facing him. Always cautious, James was looking at it real hard. He was trying to determine if there was someone in the car that he knew.

As they came alongside each other, both cars were barely moving. James recognized the three occupants as people he had known for years. They were not masked up at all. James knew at that very moment what was going to happen, why they were sent there. He had just grabbed his mobile phone to ring the club. He dropped it, and as he started to lean down to get it, one of the three men pulled out a gun. *Bang, bang, bang.* James ducked right down, as his phone was on the floor. He picked the phone up. What seemed to be minutes was only really a few seconds.

They were well past James's car by now. They drove off not looking back, obviously thinking they had killed him. They believed they had their victory. They had shot Big Jim. Maybe that's why they didn't hide their faces—that's how sure they were that they were going to kill him.

James dialled the number to the Devil's Dogs clubhouse. One of the club men answered the phone. "I've been shot!" James yelled down the phone.

The man on the other end said, "Fuck me! Are you okay, dude?"

"Yep," said James.

"Who was it?" the man on the other end asked James.

James rattled off the names of the three men who had been sent to kill him—men he once called his friends, men he had history with. He had been shot, but it wasn't fatal. They had hit him in the arm, and a bullet had grazed his face. With his heart racing, James sped to the clubhouse. As he arrived, the gates were opened, and he was met by a huge number of men. The club was abuzz by this time. James jumped out of the car. His arm was bleeding, and blood was pouring out of his face. The old Ford still had bullets in her where the gunman had fired and missed.

He rang Natalie, as she had heard the gunshots from the house. It had happened right in front. "Fuck me," she said, "are you okay, babe?"

"Yeah, ring you later," he said. "On my way to the hospital. Take the kids and go to your auntie's."

James was met by about twenty bikies. They were pissed right off. James told them who it was, as he had seen their faces The bikies were all yelling and screaming about the three men. "This is it. This is fuckin' war!"

The police came and were trying to talk to James. He told the police to piss off. The police then warned the group of men, "Don't you take the law into your hands. We will handle this." The police were trying desperately to keep some control of the situation.

James was taken to the hospital not by ambulance but by a group of twenty men who escorted the car the whole way. The police were not far back. They knew what this meant. It was going to get messy.

A friend who had a business not far from the clubhouse rang me and told me what had happened. James had managed to call him and ask him to contact me. I quickly rang Mum. Telling her without making her hysterical was really hard. "James has been shot but he's okay, Mum," I said. Mum was still recovering from major surgery. She'd had an ulcer burst a few months earlier and nearly died. She wasn't well at all.

I arrived at Mum's and two of my cousins met me there. I left my baby with Mum. I was still shaking; my adrenaline was pumping. I could not believe that he had been shot.

My cousins and I got into my car and drove off down the road. When we arrived at the hospital, it was buzzing. There were police everywhere, along with TV crews, newspaper reporters, and bikies. They were at the door of emergency, not letting anyone pass. The police were trying to talk to James inside. The bikies were arguing with the police. I walked over, and a couple of them recognized me. Grabbing me by the arm as we got to the entrance, they told me he was okay. "We're here," they assured me, "no one is going to get past us." They were trying to reassure me that James would be safe. They let my cousins and me in.

I burst into tears to see him laying there with tubes coming out of him. The doctors were having trouble trying to access him, as the bikies inside were not moving. He was talking to a couple of the boys, obviously about what had gone on. They were talking about the three men who had done it. I could hear part of the conversation; they were blabbering about what they should do. The bikies were saying to James, "Don't worry, mate, their day will come, when they least expect it."

He yelled across the room to me to come over to him. He grabbed me and cuddled me, and he said, "I'm okay. They missed." My cousin was crying as well. Her brother was talking to James, asking him if he was okay and where did he get shot. He asked James who it was, and James named the three men. Two were members of the Satan's Sons, and the other an associate of theirs.

The men standing guard were very angry. They were ranting and raving about the Satan's Sons, saying that they were all dogs. "Maybe we need to do something," one of them said. This was not good. The poor doctors and nurses were trying to work. The men were not very cautious and were causing more problems than there needed to be.

My cousins and I eventually left the hospital. Back at my mum's house, I explained that James was okay and that he would go back to the club later. Whilst he was in the hospital, the Devil's Dogs would keep guard on him. They were going to have to teach these pricks a lesson. They kept on and on about it.

After James was released, he was escorted to the clubhouse by a group of men. After James arrived, nearly all the members were called to an urgent meeting. The club was assessing what damage had been done and what they were going to do. James warned the Devil's Dogs that whatever they did, the Satan's Sons would respond back tenfold. The tit-for-tat would just keep going.

It was believed that James had given information to the Devil's Dogs about the Satan's Sons. But even though they did what they did to him, he said nothing. In that world, people should have understood that even though James was not involved with the Satan's Sons anymore, he still held on to the vow of silence. Even stupid bikies should have realized that. If he had broken that vow and given information to the Devil's Dogs, how would they ever be able to trust him?

But I think that's where common sense did not happen. We really need to allow for the most stupid of people. James never, not even once, told the Devil's Dogs anything about his old club. He knew of the consequences if he did.

In September that same year, the bikie war exploded into the local magistrate's court. Two members of the Devil's Dogs pulled up. Both were dressed real casual, in jeans and flannel shirts. They parked right out in front of the building, not caring about any consequences. As they casually walked into the building, people just stopped and stared; both men were very recognizable. They pushed through the door to the courtroom, telling the security guards to fuckin' get out of their way, and marched in.

Court was in session. The judge looked up as both men entered, because of the noise at the doorway. One of the Devil's Dogs members stood by the door, not letting the guards in. The other walked up to an associate of the Satan's Sons, one of the men who had been involved with the shooting of my brother. He began rapidly punching the man in the face. The associate just stood there as both men yelled abuse, calling him a fuckin' dog and asking, "How tough are you now?" He did not even fight back.

The judge was shouting, "Order in the court!" But with no regard for the law, the men ignored him. The judge was banging his hammer. "Order, I said!" The men then opened the door, leaving their victim bleeding, and walked out. One of them called as they left, "You are marked, you fuckin' low dog."

A security guard ran into the courtroom to assist the man who had been bashed. The judge called "Order!" and asked the man if he wanted to lay charges.

The man just said, "No, I do not want to lay charges. I don't know what you're on about, sir."

The men had reached the street. They strolled over to their car and simply drove off. They were pumped and did not care about the consequences. It just felt fuckin' great.

James, Milo, Jenny, and Mum were constantly in and out of court. They were always running into a few of the police officers involved in the task force, a senior police officer who hated my brother and caused all sorts of grief. He was in court one day, and as James and everyone passed, he deliberately tripped us. James grabbed him and punched him. A large group of officers and security grabbed James and separated them. The police officer was taunting me, wanting James to explode.

Maria told James to calm down. The police took James away and were going to charge him with assault on a police officer, but Maria weaved her magic and told the police that it would result in her client charging the police officer. After a few hours, it was decided that James would not be charged.

They were constantly harassing James and my family. They were on a mission to break him. The police officer would always taunt Jenny as well. Jenny would just fire up and screech terrible things at him. The police officer seemed to love it.

A month later, the violence reached the inevitable fatal scenario. Satan's Sons member Joel Turner was driving on his way to work when he was ambushed by a shooter waiting in the bushes near the highway off-ramp. His car was sprayed with bullets as he drove past, resulting in Turner running off the road. He was seriously injured, with spinal damage where the bullets had hit him. It was all over the news that the bikie war had hit a new low. The police were struggling to keep this under control.

This was going to create more problems than anyone could imagine. James warned the Devil's Dogs to expect a payback. He warned them that the Satan's Sons president would be very vindictive over this. Of course, there is another theory. Joel Turner was a long-time member of Satan's Sons. He was one of many who had disagreed with what the club had done to James. Maybe they shot their own man to make the war happen. No one will ever really know the truth.

The very next day, Devil's Dog member Peppe Russe was shot dead in his car in a small industrial area on the other side of town. Fellow gang member Big James Avery was shot in the arm. All hell broke loose. The Devil's Dogs all came to the spot where Peppe was. There were police everywhere, as well as bikies who were very angry and upset. The police were doing their best to keep this under control. It was a very well-planned attack.

Even to this day, I'm not really sure why they killed Peppe. I wonder if they got their intel wrong. They were told that Peppe was with Big James, and I wonder if they thought that my brother James was in the car. Maybe no one informed the shooters and they just took an opportunity. Who knows. The whole shooting of that poor man was not fair. Even though I have no time for the Devil's Dogs, they had not killed anyone. Where was this going to end? James said the police had come to the clubhouse and made it very clear they would not stand for retaliation. They wanted to deal with the situation.

This was to be a very sad time for my brother. He blamed himself for Peppe's death, and he lived with that guilt every day. He was devastated. Other members of the Devil's Dogs blamed my brother as well, and James found the guilt too much. He wondered why like everyone else. But James sunk into a real low when he looked at Peppe's wife and daughter. It was too much.

The police were putting a huge amount of pressure on James, constantly annoying him. They wanted the murderer of Peppe Russe, and they believed the gunman who shot my brother was the same one. James would just say, "No, I'm not doing this." He refused constantly to name the person.

James was pulled into the CCC and was asked to name the shooter. He kept refusing, resulting in days of interrogation and fines. He paid thousands of dollars out because he would not answer. A media person who my brother had been friends with was also questioned, but it was mainly guilt by association.

After the shooting, James needed some stability, so he bought a coffee shop near the city. He told Maria that Jenny would be working there with him, as he could trust her. James was still living with Natalie and the two children, but they had moved again. James bought yet another house not far from Mum and not far from his first house. Natalie was comfortable there. James made sure they had all they needed. But he was a torn man. He'd actually fallen in love with Maria and wanted to be with her, but what about the other two? Could his life get any more screwed up? What was he thinking?

He was in a real mess, and he decided enough was enough. He told Natalie it was over—he was leaving. It tore him apart, because he loved his two children, but he just did not love Natalie anymore. She was very angry. She had stood by him through some terrible times, but that's life.

He moved out and back to his first house. He was now a bit paranoid. He had bars and wood put over his windows at the front off the house. A huge brick wall surrounded the house. He had alarms put in and cameras. The death of Peppe still was shaking him.

Mum worked at the coffee shop sometimes, and I would help out when I could. My partner owned a shop up the road, and we lived nearby. James told Jenny that Maria was just helping him with the business. To keep the women from running into each other, James told Maria not to come to the shop when Jenny was there. So it was cruising along for a while.

The police again were stepping up the pressure. Eventually, a member of the Satan's Sons was charged with the murder of Peppe Russe and the wounding of James Avery. They also charged him with the attempted murder of my brother. The police had some work to do, as no one was talking on either side. They kept at James to testify.

Stan and Garry were the two detectives in charge of this mess. I did not really like Stan; he just annoyed me. He was a middle-aged man, tall and slender in build. He had an annoying way about him. Garry, now, he was a bit of all right, a tall man with a solid build and a shaved head. Whenever I would see him, I would think, *Mmm, he's okay.* James would just look at me and shake his head *no don't even bother.* I thought, *oh well, I can still look.* One can always imagine.

They organized another raid on Mum's house, another search warrant. It was summer. Mum had not been home long when there was a knock at the door, and Paul went to see who it was. He was told to open the door, that they were police, and that they had a warrant.

Paul replied, "I'll just go and get the boss."

The police officer yelled at him, but Paul is partly deaf anyway, so he just walked away. Mum went to the door and asked, "What do you want?"

They replied, "We're from organized crime, and we have a search warrant. Open the door."

Mum argued with them for a few minutes but eventually let them in. It was just getting dark and still really hot. The police all barged in, getting Paul and our sister to sit on the lounge floor. Mum then walked out of the house and turned the power off. Stan asked her what she was doing, and Mum replied, "It's my power, I can turn it off if I want." They had a huge argument. He warned her he would go and get generators if necessary, and they would be there longer. Mum finally turned the power back on and went back inside. She really only did it to annoy them.

The police officer then read the warrant to Mum and asked her to tell them her name. Mum replied, "No, you are standing in my house with a search warrant, and you are asking me to give you my name? No."

They again said, "Tell us your name."

"No. You have my name on that bit of paper. It tells you who I am."

"We need you to tell us who you are."

"No," she said again.

Paul yelled out, "Just tell them!"

Mum can be very stubborn. She just kept saying, "No, you know who I am." But eventually she did tell them her name. She realized this was going to be a very long night. They searched the house and found nothing. They were there for hours but sadly left empty-handed. Mum was furious. This was not fair; she had done nothing wrong.

James's life was heading down a path he couldn't turn back from. Every time the police went to the coffee shop, Jenny would greet them at the counter. Garry and Stan would enter, and Garry would say, "Good morning, Jenny, how are you?"

Jenny's response was, "What do you dog cunts want?"

Garry would say with a laugh, "Nice to see you too, Jenny. Always a pleasure."

James always knew by her tone who was at the counter. He would come out and say, "Fellows, you're wasting your time."

This was a constant event. The more pressure was put on James, the more he would hold steady like a rock. He would simply say, "Not interested, go away, and leave me alone. Go on and annoy someone else." But like clockwork, they'd be back again.

James's coffee shop was near an old people's meeting place. The old ladies would call in for coffee, and they loved having a chat. My brother loved talking to them. We can learn a lot from our elders. The boys from the Devil's Dogs would often call in for a catch up. They would sit outside in full view, but the old people did not pay any attention to them. Maybe that was the attraction.

James's life was going through some sort of transition. A Satan's Sons member was heading for trial, but with no witnesses, the police case was really useless. More pressure was put on James, who was still facing drug charges with Milo and Jenny.

More raids took place. This time, they raided about five different places at once. They had search warrants for all. Mum's house again got searched; James's own house, although no one was there; Jenny's house; the coffee shop; and my own house. The pressure was mounting. The police thought if they continued with the pressure, James would maybe help them. No chance.

At Mum's, they took away furniture and personal belongings. They asked Mum, "Do you have plants here?"

Mum replied, "Yeah, sure, out the back."

Twenty officers searched out the back. They searched everywhere. No luck. They came back in and asked again, "Where are the plants?"

Mum replied, "There are palms, roses, and …"

They stopped her before she could finish. They knew where she was headed with the line she was taking. They took Mum, our sister, and Paul to police headquarters for questioning. Mum rang me to come there to be with my young sister.

But I had other problems. James was at my house. He had been around the corner when all the raids started. I said, "What's going on?"

He replied, "They are just trying to be smart-arses."

Jenny rang and said, "James, they're here." There were police all over her yard. They had blocked her street off and were at the door with a warrant. Jenny was screeching at the police, calling, "Dog cunts, fuck off!" They insisted she open the door.

Jenny went out the back, and there was a policewoman following her around. Jenny said, "You, right there, dog cunt." The policewoman was relentless. Jenny turned on the hose and started to squirt the policewoman. The policewoman went to grab the hose and Jenny jumped at her and began to wrestle her to the ground. They were rolling around the back lawn, Jenny still squirting the hose, calling the police names. This went on for a few minutes.

Another couple of police officers grabbed Jenny, who was covered in mud. They warned her she would be charged if she did not settle down. They searched her whole house and removed some objects. Then they took Jenny into custody. Jenny's children and mother were not charged.

Back at my house, James had asked me to drive down to his shop and see if they were still there. He did not want to ring because the phones were tapped. So I grabbed my baby and made my way out the front, locking James inside. Putting my baby in the car, I got in and pulled out. I had only gone about twenty metres when I was set upon. In front of me, behind me, and to both sides of me, there were police everywhere. I stopped the car and wound down my window.

I said, "Do you mind? Who do you think you are?"

Stan approached my car. "Get out," he said.

"No," I replied.

He opened my car door. "Get out, or I will pull you out."

I was thinking, *What have I done to deserve to be spoken to like this?*

Garry approached the car and said, "Clara, please hop out and open your boot."

My neighbours had now all come out, as I live across from a heap of units. People were standing in the street.

One of my neighbours made his way across the road. When he was stopped by the police, they asked him, "What do you want?"

He replied, "I was just coming to see if Clara wanted me to take the baby."

They let him approach me. I was arguing with them about the boot. The tactical response team was there with their vests on and guns out. *My goodness*, I thought.

I gave my neighbour my baby, and he and his wife took her to their house. Meanwhile, my house and car were surrounded by police. I asked Stan, "Where is the warrant? You can't do this."

"Open the boot," he said in a very angry voice.

I opened the boot. "Satisfied?" I said, as it was empty.

"Open your front door, or we will break it down."

I again asked, "Why? Where is your warrant? You have no right to do this."

As I made my way to the front door, James opened it and yelled, "Clara, don't worry about it," and we all went in. Stan got James to sit down at my table.

James was seriously pissed off. His whole family had been harassed, and it looked like Mum was going to be charged. Stan told James everyone would be charged with something if he did not cooperate. He told James that all he had to do was to give them names and they would stop.

James just said, "Fuck you. I will never tell you anything. You are wasting your time."

I was talking to the police in my kitchen. They advised me that Mum had been charged with conspiracy to grow and supply marijuana to the Devil's Dogs bikie gang. I replied, "You're fuckin' kidding." I stormed into the dining room and said to James, "Mum is being charged now. Just tell them. They know anyway."

But he refused. He said, "It doesn't matter what you do, I will never tell you."

Stan scratched his head, flicked his hair to one side, and said to James, "We can help you. But you need to testify."

James again said, "Fuck off."

They put James in handcuffs and marched him out of my house in front of my neighbours. They put him into the car and took him to police headquarters, where he was interviewed again. They kept at him, but he said nothing. They were never going to get him to testify.

I rang my partner, Carl, and he came home. I explained to him what was going on. It was a real mess. He really had no answers for me. I then rang one of my cousins. I explained that I had to go to the police station, could she watch my baby? When my cousin arrived, I headed off, not knowing what to expect.

When I arrived at the police station, I was escorted upstairs where my younger sister was. They had to wait to interview her, as she was underage. I walked in and sat down. Before they began, I said to my sister, "Just tell them your name, age, and where you live. Nothing more."

They got angry with me. "Too bad," I said. "She is only a kid. She doesn't know anything."

They had interviewed Paul, and I think he irritated them more as, being deaf, he really could not hear what they were saying, so in the end they let him go. Mum was being interviewed in the next room. James and Jenny had been sent to the local lock-up.

In Mum's interview, they were asking her what she had been growing in the cupboards. Mum replied strawberries. "Bloody big ones, I might add." They were on about James, asking Mum about his girlfriends. Mum sighed, "Well, you know, I think my son may be gay."

The police just shook their heads. "What do you mean?" they asked.

Mum again said, "I don't know. I just think he's gay."

The police could see it was a waste of time interviewing Mum. They kept at her for over four hours of constant interviewing, and then finally Mum was charged and taken to the local lock-up where James and Jenny were. Mum explained to the police that she was claustrophobic and would find it difficult to be put in a cell. They decided to put her in with James.

As Mum walked past the cells, Jenny jumped up onto the wire and said, "Please don't leave me here."

Mum said, "Bail is on its way."

Jenny was like a wild ape, clinging to the wire, shaking on it. There were other people in her cell with her—disgusting people. There was vomit and urine on the ground. The stench as you walked past was hideous. The walls were marked, and there were prisoners screaming out as Mum walked by. Jenny kept yelling, "Don't leave me here! Please, get them to let me come with you."

As Mum walked into the cell with James, he just looked up. He was a shattered man. Mum sat down and said, "It's okay, mate." James put his finger up to his nose to tell Mum not to say anything. Mum said again, "It's okay."

They sat there for hours. Mum told me later, "You can do a lot of soul-searching in a place like that. You have nothing else to do but think." Mum could hear Jenny still yelling down the passageway, but there was nothing she could do. Time just goes by so slowly when you are waiting.

Milo was pulled in again and held at the lock-up. I arrived and walked up to the counter. I explained I was there to bail out three members of my family. The policeman looked puzzled. "Three members, you said?"

"Yeah, that's right. James Jobson, my mum, and Jenny."

"Just take a seat. We're waiting for the Justice of the Peace to arrive."

As I was sitting there, I looked outside. There were TV crews and reporters from the local newspaper. *My God, don't they ever stop?* I thought.

As time went by, Milo's brother arrived as well to bail Milo out. What seemed like forever was really not. Finally they called me up. The Justice of the Peace was an elderly man—short, plump, and balding, with large black glasses. I sat down as he was reading the paperwork in front of him. He kept looking over his glasses at me.

He cleared his voice. "Do you understand what it means to bail someone out?"

"Yes," I replied.

"These are serious charges. Are you sure you want to do this?"

I replied again, "Yes, they're my *family*."

He was writing something down; I wasn't sure what it was. He asked again, "All three?"

"Yes," I said, "all three."

As he finished the paperwork, he rang for a police officer and said, "The paperwork is done, they're ready to go."

Milo's brother was next. He wasn't in there that long, as he only had one to bail out. He looked at me and said, "This is just never going to end, I gather." He had bailed his brother out quite a bit.

Finally, after what had been an extremely long day, Mum, James, and Jenny walked out from behind a huge door. I grabbed Mum by the arm. She did not look well. James started to talk to Milo's brother. Next minute, Milo walked out as well. "Isn't this just crap?" Milo started voicing anger at the fact that they had been dragged back in.

James grabbed me by the arm and said, "Take the old girl home. I'm real worried about her." Mum was a bit wobbly on her feet. It had been an extremely trying day. "Take Jenny home as well," he asked me. James looked drained. He was now very concerned. They had pushed him into a corner, and the light was fading.

*Where to from here?* I wondered. They had made it so that there was no way out, but James was stubborn, and there was no way they would ever break him. As we went to go outside, cameras were in our faces, bulbs flashing. Putting our heads down, we walked past them all. Maria was there waiting for James and Milo. The TV crew just wanted a story. James told them to fuck off. Milo loved the media attention, so he started talking to them. James finally left with Maria. Milo was in his element.

There were going to be months of this going to court. It was a nightmare. Mum had been charged as a co-conspirator to supply and sell marijuana to the Devil's Dogs. It was sickening that the police would go as far as they did. James still would not tell them anything; he just wanted to be left alone. Unfortunately, this was not going to happen.

Every day they would call into his coffee shop, and every day they were greeted the same way. The coffee shop could be full of people, and Jenny would still speak to them as she always had.

"Good morning, Jenny, how are you?"

"You dog cunts fuck off and leave us alone."

"Glad you are good."

"James, the dog cunts are here."

The people standing in the coffee shop would simply say nothing. Jenny would go right back to serving them.

The police kept up the pressure. At Peppe Russe's funeral, James was a truly broken man. He kept on blaming himself for Peppe's death. But in hindsight, it wasn't his fault at all. The funeral had bikies from everywhere. The bikies of some of the other clubs also attended. As usual, police had to be there in force.

The bikes filled the air with loud thundering noise, smoke streaming out of exhaust pipes. The bikies were all patched up, riding behind the hearse, breaking the law again by wearing no helmets. Police were everywhere, and they did not want more violence. Letting the bikies ride helmet-free saved altercations that were not necessary.

The wake was invite-only back at the clubhouse. It went on for days. Drug-fuelled and drunken men are not a good sight at all. James was still angry with what had been going on.

Finally, the first court appearance came for James, Milo, Mum, and Jenny. We arrived at the district courthouse. This was only a hearing, but as we stepped out of the lift to the courtroom, there was officers everywhere. They had a metal detector and were scanning us all. I was thinking, *How rude*. James just pushed me forward.

The police were frisking us. Milo was behind me, drugged as usual and his normal bombastic self. "Ahh, would you like me to do that, Clara?"

I just looked at him and replied, "No, I think they've got it."

He loved all the attention and notoriety that went with who he was. James could not be bothered. We all sat down. The next minute a group of bikies entered and sat at the back, trying very hard to look intimidating.

They were large men dressed in black jeans and T-shirts, as they were not allowed to wear the patches into court. They were being loud and rude.

Maria arrived, as she was our lawyer. She spoke to James and Milo about what was going to happen. They were all called up, and the charges were read out. *What a bloody joke*, I thought. *Mum being charged alongside bikies. So very sad.*

Mum hung onto the side of the table, as she was feeling weak. Her legs could barely hold her up. She was pale and very shaky. The judge just gave us another date, and we were allowed to go.

James would come over to my house. He was just so messed up. I asked James, "Why don't you just tell them what you know? Then it is done."

"No way," he said. "This is not going to go the way the police think it will."

I asked, "Why are you protecting these people? Why don't you just tell the police who they were?"

James answered, "I cannot do that. Even though I'm not part of that club anymore, I gave my word. I cannot tell the police."

As the next few months went by, James moved again. He moved to the north side of town. He and Maria bought a house there where he would live.

His relationship with Natalie had broken down even more. Natalie was making it hard for him to see his children. Maria was now also doing family court work for my brother. His relationship with Maria was growing, and he now had introduced her to his children. He needed her more than ever.

Another court case, this time family court, fighting with Natalie about the children. It seemed that every part of James's life involved courthouses. James would tell me sometimes his head felt like it was going to explode. I think that's why he enjoyed smoking pot, just to relax.

James had been busy, and on some nights he would sleep at the coffee shop. I think it was just a place where he could be alone. All the court cases were marching on. Finally, after months and months, Emery—the Satan's Sons member accused of killing Peppe and injuring James—was to stand trial. A date had been fixed. James was under enormous stress again. As the date got closer, threats were being made via other people to James to watch his back.

They were also threatening other members. They had not let go of the fact that two men had belted the associate in court. It was now really scary for all of them. James had decided to sleep at the coffee shop again. What he didn't know was that someone had put a bomb there. In the early hours one morning, it went boom. James was asleep on the floor. Glass shattered as the door blew off. The sound itself was terrifying. People reported hearing it nearly one kilometre away.

The counters had been destroyed, and everything was a total mess. James was clearly shaken. "Fuck!" he yelled. He ran out the front to see if he could see anyone. No one was there. The people who had planted the bomb did not know James was asleep inside.

Sirens were now blaring. The police and fire department were on their way. James grabbed his phone and made a call to Maria, and then he rang me. I was sound asleep. I heard the phone and jumped up out of bed. "Hello, who is it?"

"It's me." I knew my brother's voice, but it had a slight tremor in it.

"What's wrong?" I said.

He answered, "They've blown the coffee shop up. It's fucked."

"Are you okay?" I asked.

He said, "Yeah. Look, cops are all over this. Can you ring Garry for me? Tell him what's happened and to get here."

"Are you sure you're okay?"

"Yeah, just ring Garry."

I immediately found Garry's number and rang, telling him what had happened. Garry had already heard and was on his way. I rang Mum to tell her what had happened. They thought I was in labour, as I was about eight months pregnant.

In the morning, I caught up with James. He was tired and stressed. He pulled me to one side. "See, this is what is going to happen if I say one word," he told me.

"What do you mean?" I asked.

James replied, "This is a warning." He was starting rant and rave. I just zoned out. This was an impossible situation for my brother. I realized that even though he would never have told the police, the Satan's Sons were just making sure. The message was loud and clear.

The Devil's Dogs member's trial began. The DPP put forward its case. James was called to the stand and asked repeatedly about the attempt on his life. James refused to answer any questions at all. He was later dismissed as a hostile witness. James just wanted no part of it. The police case just fell apart. They had nothing.

Following the acquittal, Milo had a bomb sent to his house as well. They were letting him know he was next. He finally moved his family out and into protection. Again, the situation was grim. Was there ever going to be an end?

James, Milo, Mum, and Jenny were back in court again, the district court. Here we go again. Again we were scanned at the entrance. This particular day, Milo was off his head on drugs, just acting like a complete idiot. He was dressed in jeans and a bright red shirt with big white flowers on it. The shirt was opened, and he was caring a man bag. As I was being scanned, he was behind me yelling, "Clara, how would you like me to be rubbing up your legs? We could get all hot and steamy." I just ignored him. It was all you could do. He was being scanned and just liked being a dickhead.

We were all sitting, waiting. It was a lady judge, a stern-looking woman with brownish hair pulled back. She wore glasses that sat on her nose. Every now and then, when the noise level rose, she would look over her glasses at us. Milo was in the back row talking very loudly to other members of the club. There were again about twenty men there in the back rows. Milo was blabbering about his night-time conquests and what he had been doing with them. His voice was very loud. The judge lady would stop talking and look up. "Mr. Calabrese," she would say, "this is a courtroom. We are not interested in what you did last night, or any other night for that matter."

He would reply, "Yeah, okay." Then he would continue his conversation with the bikies. This time his phone rang. It was in the bottom of his man bag. He was tumbling through everything, looking for it.

The lady judge again stopped and looked over her glasses. "Mr. Calabrese, is that your phone ringing?"

He replied, "Yeah, I think so."

"Why haven't you turned it off?"

Milo replied, "Don't know, your honour."

As the phone continued to ring, the judge became impatient. "Mr. Calabrese, turn your phone off or I will have it removed."

"Yeah, trying, can't find it," Milo said, still rummaging through his bag.

The lady judge said in a stern voice, "You were meant to turn it off at the door. Can you not read? And can you again please be quiet? This is a courtroom, not a bar." The phone kept ringing, but finally he turned it off.

James just rolled his eyes at me and shook his head. He put his head down. He did not want to go back to prison. As the judge proceeded, Milo again got loud, laughing and making jokes about the female prosecutor.

The judge was losing her patience. "Mr. Calabrese, if you do not quiet down, I will have you charged with contempt. You have been warned for the last time. Do you understand, Mr. Calabrese?"

"Yeah, yeah, I'm hearing you, yeah, your worship."

Finally, after what seemed like a very trying morning, the lady judge called them all up. The charges were read. They were pleading guilty to the lesser charges. James just wanted this to be over. He was concerned. His face and head were red. His blood pressure must have been at an all-time high. The judge was letting them sweat it out.

The judge asked Mum, "Why are you pleading guilty when they found nothing at your house? There is no evidence to support these charges." James hung his head. He was so very sad. This was another situation he could not fix, another reminder of a life gone by. This whole mess just would not go away.

Mum had been advised that if she pled guilty to growing two plants, the charges would be dropped against James for conspiracy, Not a good thing, but there was no other way. Poor Mum stood up, she was shaking. James felt shame and anger. The police just did this to make him break. Now the old girl would have a conviction for drugs.

The judge was looking puzzled at Mum again. She said again, "Why are you doing this, Mrs. Jobson?"

Mum choked back tears and answered, "I just want this over with. I just want to plead guilty and get on with it."

"Right," the lady judge said. "So be it." James's face was red. He was exploding on the inside, without saying a word. He did not want to go back to prison.

The lady judge spoke to James and Milo. She could see James was very agitated. His face was red. He was moving around a lot, and his hands were fidgeting. It was like he was about to explode.

The judge said, "I will tell you that I'm not going to send you to prison for this." James's body language spoke volumes. His shoulders relaxed a little as he sighed. His face returned to a normal shade, and he stopped moving around so much.

The lady judge then went back to Mum. "Mrs. Jobson, I'm going to fine you two hundred dollars for two plants that were never found. Are you guilty?"

"Yes," said Mum.

"Okay. Two hundred dollars it is." The judge just shook her head and murmured, "This is unbelievable. I do not understand you, Mrs. Jobson."

Mum nearly fell over, she was so stressed. Mum grabbed hold of the table to steady herself. Jenny was fined about ten thousand dollars and put on probation. Then came James and Milo. The lady judge made passing comments about Milo's behaviour. She was clearly not impressed. She told him to button his shirt and have respect in her courtroom. She kept on telling Milo that he really needed to be behind bars, that he was simply not a nice person. But she finally fined them, and they were free to go.

James was so relieved. He took this huge breath to calm down. He shook his head at Milo, who again had started being loud and making passing comments.

As we all walked out of the courtroom, we headed for the lift. It was me, James, Jenny, Mum, and Milo, plus four other bikies. Much to my disbelief, the lady prosecutor got into the lift with us. As she stood there very quietly, one of the bikies made conversation about her to the other men. "I think you need a good fuckin'. How about me and the boys come around later?" James just looked at me and shook his head. I wonder sometimes why it was that he wanted to be one of them.

The lady prosecutor just stood there. She did not even utter a word. They just kept at her all the way to the bottom. I bet she was glad to get out of the lift. As she walked away, they were still yelling things at her. It is a wonder they did not get arrested. As we all got out, I could not wait to be rid of their company. They were just despicable.

Now with all the court cases behind us, James was sighing with relief. It was time to get a new business. The coffee shop was gone, so James needed another job. He bought a lawn-mowing business, which suited him, as he did not have to deal with many people.

James was still very paranoid about the Satan's Sons. He did not know where all this was going to end. All he knew is that he had to be extra careful and watch his back, because he felt that he could not trust any of them.

Life was slowly getting back to normal for me and for James. And then one day, James rang and said, "I need to see you."

I was home waiting when he arrived. He was stressed again. "What now?" I said.

"Fuck, you know, why people involve me in their shit I don't understand," James said. He was ranting about how people should clean up their own mess.

I was puzzled. "What?" I said.

"Fuckin' women," he said. He put his head down into his hands and then said, "I'm going to tell you a story. I really need to talk to someone."

I was interested, so I sat there.

James seemed to be thinking about where to start the story he wanted to tell me. His face was worried. Then he started. He said a mate, Tony, who he had known for many years, the one with bipolar disorder, had been accused of raping one of the bikie boys' girlfriends. He had been working in one of the pubs in the mining town and met this woman. She had been a barmaid or dancer. I think Tony had picked up this woman, and they had an affair. James wasn't sure how long the affair went on; he really didn't care.

The woman's boyfriend at the time was a high-ranking bikie. The woman got caught out; someone had seen her go off with this other man. "She told her fella that my mate had raped her," James said.

I was stunned. "Did he rape her?" I asked.

James said, "No, she just said that because she got caught fuckin' another bloke. I'm really sure it's being going on for some time. She is just a dirty slut."

"So why are you involved?" James looked so sad. He was clearly torn. "What do they want from you? Why doesn't the woman go to the police?" These were all questions that could be answered, but he could not answer them. "Why doesn't her fella just deal with it?" I asked.

"Exactly," said James. Finally a response. James was overwhelmed with emotion. He hated the woman anyway. James always thought that her first child belonged to Tony. She had been having the affair that far back. But James had decided a long time ago to just forget it. He did not want to be involved with other people's drama.

He was just sitting there. It was quite disturbing. He was miles away. I could see a sadness in his face that I had not seen since we were children.

James then said to me, "I have been told to do something that I know is wrong. I don't want to be involved, but they have dragged me in, and now I really do not know what to do." I asked him to explain to me what it was they wanted him to do.

He said they had called him to a meeting at the clubhouse and told him that he was sworn to loyalty to them. He was a patch member. They were his brothers, Then they told him about the rape and what was going to be done to Tony. James asked, "Why doesn't her man just go bash the bloke himself? He doesn't have to involve all of us." James was trying to get out of this situation. He hated the woman. He told her fella, "She is just a slut. Why are you wasting your time? You know she just isn't any good. In the long term, this will all come back on us." They just kept on telling James this was how it was going to be.

The senior members of the club wanted it to be handled in-house. No police. Tony had to be brought to the club for this to happen. "So what do you want from me?" James asked.

"He is your friend. You will go and get him and bring him here. He won't suspect anything if you go and get him. "

Then James asked them, "What are you going to do then?"

"Well," they said, "if you go and get him, we will bash him. But we will not kill him, because he was your friend. If you do not go and get him, we will kill him, and you being a patch member will be ordered here. You will then watch us bash him and probably kill him. This is your choice," they said to James.

"That's bullshit," he said. "I should not be involved in this."

But again, they played the card. "You are a patch member of this club. You know the rules."

James was clearly torn. The man they wanted to bash had been his friend for many years. James believed that he did not deserve this. But the club wanted it to be a warning to other women about what would happen if they got caught playing around. James said to me, "This is really fuckin' bad. I just know this is not going to end well."

I said to James, "Leave the club. They're not your friends. They would not ask you to do this if they were. They are just playing you."

James again rested his face in his hands. He was so distraught. He said to me, "They will kill him."

I asked about the woman. I said, "Can't you get her to tell the club the truth?"

James replied, "She has already been beaten over this, she is not going to 'fess up. She would be too scared to. That is why she told them he raped her." James said if they ever found out that the affair had been going on for some time, they would really be pissed. She would have to go into hiding. They would kill her. James said to me, "I hate her. I always have. She is just a dirty slut."

James then asked, "Do you still have my guns here?"

"Why?" I asked.

"I need one of them."

"Which one?" I asked.

"My pistol. My magnum. Go get it," he demanded.

"Okay." I was getting scared now. James had been backed into a corner again. There was going to be no winner here. I kept trying to talk sense into him, explaining that even though the man's done wrong, he is still your friend. If he wasn't, they wouldn't have brought you into this. He just couldn't work it out.

James stayed for a while longer and then left. He took the gun and some bullets with him. I did not see or hear from him James for a few days, so I was very worried. I rang, but no answer. *What had happened?* I wondered. *What did James do? Did he go and get the man or did he tell the club to go fuck themselves?*

A few more days passed, and James finally called. I asked, "Are you okay?"

"Not really," he said. "I feel sick inside my guts like you would not believe."

I asked James what happened. He said, "It's not good. I did something that I will probably regret for the rest of my life."

I was feeling very anxious. "Tell me you did not do it." I said. "They didn't make you, did they?" He said it was terrible. "Why, what did you do?" He said he went and got Tony. His friend thought they were just going to the club. He had no idea that the woman had told her partner that he had raped her. So he was going in blind. They arrived at the club and went in.

The man whose partner said she was raped and four other men were there. They walked up to the bar, James said. The bikie whose partner was involved started the bashing. The others joined in. They beat Tony to within an inch of his life. They used bats and fists, kicked him, spat on him. It was humiliating for Tony. He tried to explain, but they would not listen.

James said it went on and on. In the end, James pulled out his gun, clicked back, and pointed it at a senior member of the club. James yelled, "Stop. That's enough now."

The senior member was not impressed. James had violated the code. He was a club member first, and then he was a human being. They were not happy. James picked up Tony off the floor. Blood was everywhere. Tony had been beaten unconscious. The woman who caused it all just stood there. She was traumatized. She knew if they believed or listened to Tony, she would be dead.

James carried his friend to his car and drove away, knowing in his heart that things would never be the same, ever. You live by the sword, you will die by the sword. James took Tony back to his house, where he nursed his friend back to health. The damage that was done to this man was massive. It had been one of the most vicious attacks James had ever seen. James felt sick.

The club had now had an urgent meeting about what James had done. They were not impressed. Eugene, one of the senior members, was the one most pissed off, as it was him James had pointed the gun at. He needed to show he was still in charge. Over the next few days, James thought about what it was he really wanted. Was he still wanting to be part of the club? Did he still fit in?

All these questions raced around his head. Tony gained strength and finally was able to get himself up. He and James had a huge argument over it. James had taken him there and set him up for the bashing. James tried to explain the situation the club had put him in. Tony vented and told James he would never forgive him for betraying their friendship. He had betrayed their trust.

Tony said, "This will not end here, I can assure you." He kept yelling at James, telling him there would be a score to be evened and that James should watch his back.

James was shattered. He now had made enemies on both sides of the fence. This was not a good place to be in. Tony just would not listen to anything James had to say. At the same time, James was being summoned to the clubhouse. It was time for him to face the music. He arrived not knowing what was going to happen. Would they bash him the same way? To be prepared, he took his gun with him. He wasn't going to be put in a situation where he would get hurt again.

The senior member that James had pointed the gun at was really only saving face. He needed to show that what James had done was the worse betrayal of all. He vented his anger at James and asked James, "What were you thinking? The guys a fuckin' head, a mental case. He is nothing. You fucked up really bad." He just kept on venting at James.

"Enough," said James. "What do you want from me?"

They told James to think about what it was that he wanted. Did he really want to still be part of the club? Where did he see himself being in the near future?

James didn't know the answer. He was conflicted. This was a huge mess to be in.

James took some time to think about what he wanted. Maria had been on him to leave the club anyway. This was a really good opportunity for James to get out clean. *But do you ever get out really?* he thought. His children were now getting older and understanding more of what was going on. The lawn-mowing business was going well. Jenny was working with James again. How he pulled the lies off, I will never know. But then again, people only really ever see what they want. Love is truly blind.

Finally, after months of agonizing over the decision, he made it. This wasn't easy, as James had looked up to these men as his brothers. He had so much faith in them, it was scary. Brothers that would in the end let him down and put a knife in his back … or maybe even put a gun into the hand of a man who sought revenge?

A meeting was called. They were all there. Maria was also in attendance. It seemed she was always around, maybe in case they needed representation or an alibi.

James was asked to tell them what he was going to do. He stood up, took a huge breath, looked at all the men at the meeting, and said, "I'm out. It's time for me to think about my children, and what I do will influence them, so I'm out." Sambo had been the one who got James to join them, so he had to be the one to take back James's patch. They told James, "You cannot just walk away. There are choices you have to make."

James knew what the choice was. There was no way he was ever going to let them bash him, not without a fight back. The other choice was to give them his Harley, the same motorbike he'd had for twenty years, his pride and joy. This bike had been through so much with James. Maria called to James to come talk to her. She told James she would buy him another one. There was no other way.

James felt gutted. He felt betrayed again. Under great duress, he handed over his bike and gave the club back its patch. He was now free. That's what he thought, anyway. Are you really ever free? James's motorbike was sold off to a man who was later charged with the murder of a tourist, a terrible situation. If that motorbike could talk …

James remained friends with some of the men. Even though it was hard, some of the men were James's friends. But his biggest regret would come back one day, and it would cost him everything. Evil comes in many forms, and it's those terrible regrets that are the ones that can change it all. That one mistake you wish you had not made. What would be the cost? A life.

*Revenge is a dish best served cold.*

# PART THREE

## *End of the Road*

# CHAPTER 7

## *The Murder*

May 2004, five fifty in the morning—a date and time I will never forget. It was the day my whole world came crashing down. There is no one who will ever understand the pain and heartache that day held. It is embedded in my mind, my heart, and my very soul. This was the beginning of a journey that affected so many souls.

It was a normal Wednesday morning. I awoke as usual at about five thirty a.m. On went the kettle and the radio. I needed to listen to my stars at six a.m. to see what the day would hold. This was my highlight. I felt like today was going to be a good day. How wrong I was.

It was five forty-five a.m. when my phone rang. It was not unusual for me to get calls that early. On the other end was a cousin who is like a brother to me. I said, "What's going on? Why the early call?" Not for one moment did I think there was anything wrong. I thought he'd just rung early for a chat. Listening to the tone in his voice, though, I asked, "Is there something wrong?" thinking something must have happened in his life.

I got a bit of a surprise when he asked me, "Everything okay?"

*Strange sort of question*, I thought, so I answered, "All good!" I remember thinking, *I've only just got up what could be wrong? Isn't he sweet checking on me?*

The words he said in his next sentence would stay in my mind from that day to this. It was like being in a moment of time standing still, like a movie that is not moving, a moment in time where you wish for a button to put the next thirty seconds on hold. But that is not how life is. The words just came.

"There has been a shooting, there has been a fatality," he said. "Have you heard?"

*Why are you telling me that someone has been killed?* I thought. My mouth now went dry. I had a feeling in the pit of my stomach that I had not felt before. I don't know whether it was my defence mechanism that now kicked in or if it was just my old survival alert, but I had a sinking feeling come over me just like the first time he was shot. That time, though, he had survived. I thought in the back of my head, *James is invincible!*

My heart started to race. I could feel my breathing change. I was trembling. My whole body was tightening up as I spurted out "Where?"

He then said, "Inner city."

Knowing the Devil's Dogs clubhouse was near there, I asked, "Where in inner city?" I could feel an overwhelming dread come over my body, like a sinking feeling in the deepest part of your gut. Before even being told, I think somewhere deep in my subconscious his name was already there.

I tried to hold my composure for what seemed like an eternity, but it was only a few moments until he uttered the words, "At the gym."

My heart felt like it stopped for what was, again, only seconds. I had to make myself breathe. My life seemed to go in slow motion as I tried to get my head around what he had just said. I could hear the six a.m. news bulletin come on, and somewhere I could hear the news flash that there had been a shooting in the inner city. I was trying to not fall to pieces; everything seemed so surreal. I knew it was James.

My whole body started to tense; I think it was just a coping mechanism. My breathing had now become very shallow, like I was hyperventilating. At that point, I told my cousin I would ring him straight back. I needed to ring James. I needed to hear James's voice on the other end of the phone. I just wanted him to pick it up. I didn't really care about any abuse that he might vent at me for calling so early. Anything would be just wonderful at this time.

All the while, I was thinking, *Please don't let this be James.* I dialled my brother's mobile number over and over again, all the time crying, begging, *Please James just answer the phone.* Every time the phone rang out, I continued to ring. By this time, I was starting to feel what I so didn't want to. I began to get angry with him.

I was jumping up and down on the spot, banging the kitchen bench with the phone. *Bang bang bang*, I hit the bench. All the time, deep in my guts, I knew it was James. "Please God," I was now sobbing, "please not like this again. Please God, not now." My body was shaking. I started to feel like my composure was gone. I couldn't breathe, I couldn't think, I just wanted it not to be true. Again, "Please! Please God!" I was now thinking out loud.

*Who can I ring?* I rang Jenny. I asked, "Have you heard from James? I've been ringing and ringing with no answer." She said she hadn't spoke to him as yet. She was meeting him at about seven to go to work.

She could sense something was wrong by my voice, and she asked me what was going on. "Is your mum okay?" I suppose, like me, we never thought James was in any more danger, so thinking something was wrong, it must be our mum.

I remember trying very hard not to lose it and then just blurting out the words. I told her someone had been shot and killed in the inner city.

Her whole tone changed. "Where in the inner city?" she screamed.

I started to cry and felt very hopeless. Through the sobs, I told her the gym. It was like we had a telepathic connection at that point. We both knew this was not good.

"Fuck! Fuck!" Jenny kept saying.

It was that moment of truth, when denial would be a whole lot better than being faced with the horror of losing a loved one at the hand of someone else. Could you ever imagine the pain that you'd feel? It is like your heart has been ripped out of your body, and every living part of you dies for those few moments, and with every second that swishes past your head. You just can't grasp what is in your brain as it tries to digest what it can handle at that point.

Jenny said she would continue to ring James. I told her I would ring Garry. Of all the police James had ever encountered in his life, he always told me Garry was a good cop and honest. Probably the only one he had ever met.

I'd been given Garry's mobile number by James as a person to ring if there was an emergency. Was this an emergency? You'd better believe it. My head was swishing in so much emotion. I wondering if I should ring him so early in the morning. *Ring him, Clara, ring him*, I told myself. *You need somebody to help with this.* Garry had been a detective in major crimes. He had been an officer with the task force. That is how I first met him; he was investigating the bikie war that had involved James. I took a deep breath and rang Garry on his mobile.

"Hello" he said. "who is this?"

I said, "Clara Jobson, James's sister." My head was spinning, and my voice was obviously distressed. He asked me what was wrong. Trying to balance it in my head, I explained what I had heard on the radio, that there had been a shooting in the inner city. "I can't seem to find out anything." I was becoming more and more distressed. I screamed and was sobbing to him. I had awakened him with my early-morning call, so he himself had not heard the news and had no idea what I was talking about.

"I think it is James," I told him. "Can you please find out? I didn't know who else to call. Please, can you call somebody, anybody? They will tell you. Please, Garry."

He was obviously up and out of bed now, trying to get his head around what I had been ranting. I explained that after my cousin rang, I had been trying James's number. Even Jenny couldn't get hold of him. God! There are James's children and my mother and my sister who have to be told if it is James. "Please," I said, "before the media go wild, there are people who love him, and finding out via the news would be terrible."

He cleared his voice and said, "Calm down, Clara." He hung up but promised to ring back straight away.

My distress was now very real. I rang central police. Crying, and in a broken voice, trying to speak through my sobs, I told them who I was. "My name is Clara Jobson. My brother is James Jobson. There has been a shooting at an inner-city gym. I think it is my brother. Can you help me?" All the while I just wanted it not to be my brother.

When the policeman on the other end said that he couldn't help me, I began to scream and cry uncontrollably. "Please!" I said. "I just want to know if it is my brother." I could barely speak clearly; I was shaking with fear. My whole body was trembling. I told the police officer that I knew it was James, I just needed to confirm what I already knew. I was still having trouble breathing. I had pain in my chest; my head was ready to explode.

The policeman said to me, "We are not normally allowed to tell people over the phone."

I begged him, "Please, tell me, is it my brother?"

He said again that this was not protocol; it just wasn't the way the police department worked. I remember screaming at him that I didn't give a fuck about protocol or police policy. I needed him to tell me and tell me now. It seemed like fucking forever, but it was only moments. He put me on hold, and as I stood there waiting, I began to feel faint. I began to sway. Still trembling, now feeling physically sick, I begin to dry retch. Waiting for the officer to get back to the phone, moments seemed like an eternity.

Finally he was back. "Miss Jobson," he said, "I have just spoken to someone, and against protocol …" I knew what was coming, but nothing ever really prepares you for that moment. The words that came next will forever haunt me. They are still here in my subconscious, and I will never forget. "Yes, it is James Jobson." It seemed like time stood still. The disbelief, but also the knowing. "I am so sorry," he continued, "so sorry to have to tell you like this."

My heart sank. I fell to my knees with tears dripping down my face. I couldn't breathe. I couldn't speak. No noise was coming from me. I was in so much pain. My heart was breaking. There are no words to describe an emotion so painful. I lay on the floor sobbing, and as the moments went by, my life went into a swirl.

The phone rang. It was Garry. As he spoke to me, I really couldn't hear. Everything seemed to stop. He said, "Clara, I have been ringing, but I have had no luck." He kept saying he would keep trying to find out who it was. He asked if I was still there. In a voice very distressed and broken, I told him it was my brother. It was James. Then I fell to pieces.

He said, "No. Fuck. Fuck me."

I said, "They told me over the phone."

He was on his way into the city to try to find out some more information. He himself couldn't make sense of this tragedy. He said he would talk to me later when he found out more details. *Does it really matter?* I thought. *Does it matter? He is dead.* I lay there sobbing, beyond any help. I just didn't know what to do. I lay there in a ball, too frightened to let any part of me go. I just couldn't feel. I couldn't think. There was no sense in anything. There was so much pain. My chest hurt. My heart was breaking. My head was totally fucked. My only brother was gone. It just didn't feel right.

*Please, God, help me. Please, God, don't let it be James.* I lay on the floor rocking, just sobbing, wailing, screaming. It all seemed so unreal, yet it was very real.

What to do? I was holding my head in my hands, trying desperately to get a handle on it. *Fuck me. What a fuckin' mess.* I just was in so much shock. The pain was so intense. It seemed like forever, but it was only a few minutes before Jenny rang me back. She said she hadn't been able to reach James. She said she rang and rang, but the phone just kept ringing. She was very agitated by now.

I was sobbing. No words were being spoken. She said, "Fuck. What? What?"

My voice seemed gone, but finally I was able to tell her, "Jenny, it was James."

The phone went silent. All I could hear was her sobbing on the other end. Her heart was breaking, and I just couldn't feel for her. My own self-preservation was kicking in. I didn't know how to deal with so much grief, let alone reach out to help someone else. I felt totally hopeless for the first time in a long time. I was trying to help myself.

I told her I would go to Natalie's to tell the children. I said I didn't want them to hear via radio or some heartless bastard. They were my family; they were James's life. I felt I should be the one to tell them. I don't know why. Maybe it was the fact that I only lived around the corner. All the while, my own children hadn't even been told that their uncle was dead. Were there any words that would help? No, none.

My relationship with Natalie had somewhat cooled since she and James had broken up, but I tried hard to still see my nephews without intruding into her life. We had a mutual understanding and had put some of our differences aside to make sure all the kids could see each other.

Jenny said she would go to my mum's and tell her. I thought, *I just cannot be the one to tell my mum.* The sadness in her life would be too much. This would be the finale of tragedies that she'd had to live through. Even now, as the dust settles, I know I should have been the one to tell my mum, but I just couldn't. I was so scared that she would die from the sheer shock. My mind was a mess. I couldn't have dealt with another situation. I sometimes feel like I was a coward, but if anything had happened to my mum, I think that would have been the straw that broke the camel's back.

As time has gone by, I think I blamed my parents instantly without realizing it until much later. I had no right to blame them, though it was easy at the time. I wanted someone to be responsible for the pain and grief I was feeling. Not for a moment did I take into account what my mother was going through; she had just lost her son. I was playing the blame game when really, it was the murderer's fault, no one else's. Who was I to do that too anybody? If I could change that, I would. I cannot, so I live with that guilt.

The phone rang again. It was my cousin. I was hysterical and beyond comforting. I told him it was James. He said, "Oh God, what about your mum, have you told her yet?"

I was trying to talk, but I just couldn't. The pain was so bad. I told him Jenny was going to Mum's. I was going to Natalie's. He said, "Fine, I will meet you at your mum's."

At that moment, my children woke up to see me curled in a ball on the ground, sobbing and rocking. I couldn't breathe or speak. They both ran to me. I didn't know what to tell them. Their poor little faces looked at me with such confusion. They automatically got upset. They had never witnessed their mother in such a state.

I eventually blurted something out. I really don't know what I actually said. I suppose that's what happens; your whole body goes on autopilot, and you melt down. It's the fight-or-flight mode, just so you can get through.

I managed to pull myself up off the ground. I grabbed my two children and held them so tight. Their poor little faces were wet with their own tears, crying for me, but they still had no idea why. That's how it is with children's unconditional love. Their mum was hurting and they were trying to understand why. I couldn't tell them. I was hollow inside—too much pain, too much sadness.

I got up and went into the bathroom. I looked at myself in the mirror. I had no recollection who I really was. I ran to the shower and just sat in the bottom, still dressed in my PJs. I let the hot water run on me, trying to get some clarity. My heart was now broken beyond repair. I kept thinking, *God, how are we ever going to get through this?* The full impact of the tragedy was now upon me.

The kids came into the bathroom and saw, to their amazement, that I was still fully clothed. One of them said, "Mummy, you are still in your clothes!" They had a bit of a giggle. Kids find the smallest things funny. I told them to undress and get into the shower like it really didn't matter, but at least it was a normal thing that they would do. I kept trying so hard to feel a bit of normal routine.

I was trying to dress myself, yelling and crying in my bedroom, just laying on my bed. My poor children looked at me in distress. A little voice asked, "Mummy, why are you so sad?" Both of them had gotten out of the shower and had put towels around themselves, and they were hugging me, wanting me to be okay and stop crying.

I just couldn't. I told them that something bad had happened, and I needed to tell them. I explained that I needed for them to be very brave for me. I kept thinking, *Is there really any easy way? No, there is not.* I sat them on the bed next to me, making sure the towels were around them, as the morning was a bit chilly.

I then said, "My brother, your uncle James, has been killed, and I am so very sad. That is why I am crying so much." Their little eyes welled up with tears. They were so young; they really had no idea of what had happened. How do you shield your children when you know that the media are going to be on this like bees to honey?

As I was getting dressed, the phone rang again. It was another cousin who used to also call me early in the morning. She knew something terrible had happened, as my voice was shaky. As I begin telling her, I realized she hadn't heard any of the radio announcements. I told her, "James has been killed. He has been shot. He is dead."

She begin to cry. "No," she said. She then told me she would ring a police officer she knew to confirm what I had already told her.

She rang me back and said, "You are right, it is James."

I eventually got myself together enough, got dressed, and got my children dressed. I even put my child in a school uniform. I don't know why; I knew they wouldn't be going to school today. But I think it was again that I needed a routine thing, because my life was out of whack. I put the children in the car and proceeded to Natalie's house, all the while trying to comprehend what had happened, trying desperately to find some clarity. What I was about to do would change people's lives forever.

It was about seven a.m. and quite cold. I had bundled the children up. I remember knocking at the door. Natalie answered. I must have looked terrible. She said, "What the hell is wrong?"

I broke down. Natalie told her older child to take all the kids into the lounge, as she had a heater on there. My heart was pounding; my voice was broken. She opened the door wider and again said, "What the fuck is wrong?" She asked if my mum was okay, automatically thinking it was Mum

I was now sobbing. I said, "No, it's not Mum, it's James. He is dead. He has been shot, and he is dead."

She grabbed me and we hugged. She said, "Fuck. Fuck. Where are all the kids?" forgetting she had sent them into the lounge room already.

I said I had to come and tell them before it went out on the radio or TV that it was James. We both were in shock. Even though Natalie was sympathetic at the moment, there was no love lost between her and my brother. They had broken up quite badly. James had left Natalie for Maria. That was just one of his regrets. So even though Natalie could show sorrow, it was probably for the fact that her two children had now lost their dad. Being a dad was the one thing James loved. The two kids were his whole life.

James had made Natalie's life a living hell, so this was probably her prayers answered. What a day for those two children. Not only had their dad been murdered, but it was also their pop's birthday, a day that will be remembered in their lives forever.

Natalie asked me about Maria. I said I hadn't heard from her—not that I thought she would be very interested, as she and James had broken up a few weeks ago. I had gone into Maria's office in March to ask for some legal advice, and she'd informed me that they had split up. I really wasn't interested, as I didn't like her much anyway. There was just something that didn't sit well with me about her. I thought she probably already knew that he was going to die, but this was only a thought, and a thought with anger attached. Again, it was like I needed someone to blame.

Maria's association with the bikies was very strong, and little did we know the depth of her anger against my brother. She'd told Sambo to have words with him over their break-up and also about some money she believed he owed her. At this point, we did not realize that this was a woman scorned. We would only find out later, as time went on, and boy was she scorned.

Natalie then said, "James always rings the children at eight a.m. I want to wait till then so I know for sure."

*Well*, I thought, *you do what you have to*, but I knew he wasn't going to ring. In my heart, I hoped everyone was wrong, but it was highly unlikely. I sat there in a heap. I just couldn't focus. I was praying that, even though I had been told by the police, maybe just maybe they got it wrong. As the time grew closer to eight o'clock, my stomach became so tight the pain was frightening. Natalie asked me if I would like a coffee, but I said no.

I felt numb and sick beyond words, knowing that in a few minutes life would change for my brother's two children. This moment would be with them forever, and no matter how I kept thinking about telling them, there wasn't any easy way. It was going to be devastating. Such tragic news was bad enough, but telling two little children was one of the worst things I would ever have to do.

The older one kept coming out of the lounge and just staring at me. It was like this poor kid knew something was terribly wrong. As time was ticking, I kept thinking that in a few moments I would help their mum tell them that their dad was dead, news that no child should have to hear.

The phone rang right at eight. My heart rose for a moment; maybe it was all a mistake. Natalie answered the phone, and I heard her say, "Maria." I knew then any hope I might have was gone. Natalie asked her, "Was it James?" I gathered the reply was yes. Natalie stood there holding the phone, and she kept saying, "Fuck. Fuck. Are you sure?"

Her conversation with Maria didn't last long. She put the phone down. The kids all came into the kitchen. The eldest knew something really bad had happened, just by me being there and in such a state.

Natalie said to her eldest son, "Your dad is dead." She screamed again, "Your dad is dead." So much for telling the child and showing some sort of compassion! He just stood there in such disbelief. Natalie grabbed and shook him. She said, "Did you hear me?" What she had said was now sinking in. She said, "Your dad has been shot, and he is dead."

The boy began to cry, saying, "No, Dad always rings at eight o'clock!"

Natalie said, "That was Maria on the phone."

The other child was in the lounge room. He really had no idea what was wrong. Natalie told him that his dad was dead, but I don't think he understood. He stayed in the lounge with my two kids. I was in the kitchen with the older one. The look on his face will haunt me forever. I still have visions about those dreadful moments. He was only eleven years old. What a terrible thing to have to go through

I sat down with my head in my hands. I couldn't focus. I could hear all this noise around me, but it had no meaning, no direction. It was just noise. Natalie came back out from the lounge, sat the older child down, and gave him a drink of water. I kept thinking, *I have to go. I have to go and face my mother. I should have been there to tell my mother and my sister.* But I had to be with James's children, just to feel them and hug them, just to try to be close to James.

All these feelings I was feeling were feelings of pain, anger, and rage. My emotions were all over the place. Natalie made me a coffee. As I was drinking it, the tears just wouldn't stop. Natalie really didn't have much more to say to me, as at that moment, her life had become her own again. There was no more James to give her hell about anything.

The phone rang. It was Natalie's dad; he had heard the news and put it all together. He was very upset, or so Natalie told me, as he loved the two children. He understood that they would need him more now than ever. Natalie's dad was a big man, but like my brother, he loved his children. He understood how much this would impact on his grandchildren's lives.

I said goodbye to Natalie and gave the children a huge hug. The older child's heart was clearly broken. Both of them loved their dad so very much. I put my two children in the car and drove off.

As we pulled up, my sister was there. So was Jenny. Their cars were parked outside. My heart was sinking. I really didn't know how to face my mum. I was blaming her for my brother's death, even though she had nothing to do with it. I was blaming my dad. I was blaming the bikies. I was blaming the world. I just wanted my brother back. I really didn't give a fuck about anyone else.

It might sound selfish, but I was in so much pain. I couldn't feel for anyone else. I had nothing in me to offer to anyone. I remember walking in, but to be honest, the next few minutes were a total blur. I remember looking at my mum. Her pain was beyond words. The heartbreak was like an open wound. It was pouring out with a sorrow that no one else could feel.

My sister walked over to me, and we hugged. I just held her so tight. She had heard it on the radio, so she came straight to Mum's. My sister was as upset as me. She was so much younger that James and I had always babied her. There were people there, but I really don't know who. I just looked at Mum and couldn't comfort her. I was still at that point of blaming her and everyone else.

My cousin turned up, and we decided that the two of us and Jenny would go to the hospital. We were told that's where they had taken James—to the inner-city hospital. There were people everywhere at my mum's, and the phone never stopped ringing. Mum told me later that she has no idea who she even talked to on that day. A few of my cousins said they would look after my kids. Being so young, they still had no idea of what was really wrong. Their nana was clearly heartbroken. She was beside herself with grief.

As we drove off, I kept thinking, *This is just so unreal.* Every radio station was reporting on this murder. It was big news, but the people rushing to make a big story of it forgot that this person has a family—a family torn apart by grief. They really didn't care. It's something for them to talk about.

We arrived at the hospital, and reporters were everywhere. Police cars and an ambulance were at the front as Jenny and I got out of the car. My cousin went off to park. As we approached, I could see there was a flurry of people. I could see police officers standing there. Maria was inside with that man Sambo. I just couldn't believe their gall.

"Why the fuck are they here?" Jenny asked me.

"I don't know," I said. I couldn't believe it either. I really didn't like Sambo. I honestly thought he was an arsehole, and as for Maria, I thought, *You bitch. Why are you here anyway?*

We were approached by two detectives who I now know as Richard and Arron. They asked who we were. I told them I was James's sister and this was James's girlfriend, and "Please can I just see my brother, please let me see him, I just want to know that it is him. Maybe it's not. Please,

please." They were trying to explain the reasons why I couldn't, but it made no sense to me.

I kept thinking, *They have no right to tell me I can't see him. I love him.* I was really scared. We were in such shock that people were all around us. There was no direction to follow, no lead to take. It was like we were stuck in a time warp, and it was pushing us through whether we liked it or not. Maria was now marching up and down, explaining to the staff that she was James's partner and had every right to see him. Sambo was just sitting in a chair looking real fuckin' smug.

Jenny grabbed me and asked me, "What the fuck does she mean that she is James's partner?"

I looked at her face and felt nothing. I knew the truth that both these woman would have to face. It was not going to be good for anybody, and I just didn't give a fuck. I couldn't do it with her at this moment. She kept grabbing me by the arm, demanding that I tell Maria that *she* was James's partner and not her. Jenny believed that Maria had never been in a relationship with James; as far as she was concerned, Maria had been nothing to him. Maria was glaring at me.

Jenny I walked up to the front desk and I asked, "Could I speak to someone?" I wanted to see my brother. I didn't care what they were saying, I just needed to see him, to hold him. I kept saying to the person behind the desk, "But he's my brother and he's all alone. Let me please go to him. I needed to see. Please." I kept it up, but they just kept telling me no, it was not possible. I stepped back.

Sambo made some sort of conversation—not that I was really interested. He said to Jenny, "Just be careful what you fuckin' say."

I glared at him and said, "Who the fuck do you think you are? Who do you think you are talking to? We are not someone you control."

He again made a comment to us both. I just looked at him and said, "Fuck you." I've never been intimidated by the whole bikie thing. I really fuckin' hate them and everything they represent. They sucked James in like they do all their members.

I asked Richard if I could I have a brief word with him. He arranged for us to go into a room with him and Arron. While we were waiting to go into the room, I was just trying to hold it all together. It was so hard.

I explained that both these women had had a long-term relationship with my brother, and neither knew about the other. Could he be a bit discreet?

I really didn't know how to handle the situation, especially at that point. I just couldn't deal with that on top of my brother's murder. Not this day. Not this moment. They were the last people I wanted to get into an all-out argument with. This was not about them; it was about my brother laying there with no one around him who loved him, no one who cared.

Richard understood. We walked back to Jenny, and then we walked into a room with her. I said to Jenny, "Tell them about the fight James had last week with Tony." James had some real concerns about the fight, as it was over a minor drug thing but had gotten out of hand. They'd had a fistfight over it in the backyard. I looked at the police and said, "It was him, I just know."

They asked us who we were talking about. Jenny and I were having a discussion between ourselves. Again they asked who it was we were talking about. We told them Tony Frankino. They asked us who he was to James and could we repeat the last name. They walked slightly away from me and Jenny and talked amongst themselves. We were discussing what we thought had happened. They walked back to us and asked us if we knew why Tony and James had argued, and were we sure that was Tony's last name.

I said, "Yes, I've known him for many years." I explained that he and James had known each other since James was seventeen. Again, they asked us what the argument was about. We didn't really want to tell them, as it was about drugs and money. We're only talking about a small amount of pot and about $1,500.

They asked us if we knew where Tony lived. Jenny said she did, and they asked her for the address. She said she didn't know it but could take them there. They again walked away and were discussing something. They walked back over to us and asked if she would go with them. She was a bit hesitant. I said to her, "Go on, show them where he lives. They don't know you. You'll be okay. I will meet up with you later at Mum's."

We walked out of the room and saw Maria and Sambo again. This time, Maria grabbed me by the arm and asked me what Jenny was doing there. I asked her to remove her hand. She kept hold, squeezing. I just pushed her off me with my other hand. I said, "She is with me."

Maria was being really nasty. She had her arms folded. Her whole demeanour was not right. She kept at me and at me, demanding answers. I just couldn't answer any of her questions, as I wasn't in the right head space. I looked at her in anger and told her to go ask Sambo. He might be able to enlighten her about Jenny.

I kept wondering, *What was my brother thinking?* I did not like Sambo. There was something that did not sit right. He stopped us and told Jenny again to watch her mouth, to be careful what she told the cops. I couldn't believe that's all he had to say. He looked at me and asked who I thought had killed James. I asked him, "Are you talking to me?"

"Yes," he replied.

"Who the fuck do you think you are?"

Again he asked, "Who do you think killed James?"

It was like this guy hadn't heard me, or really I don't think he cared what I said. In the bikie world, this was one mean man. But I really didn't bother with all his notoriety. He was still just a man.

I replied, "Tony Frankino."

He said, "What, you think that nut job shot James?"

I said, "I don't know, but my gut tells me he did."

Sambo said, "I hope it *was* the Flipper."

I said, "What the fuck are you on about?"

He mumbled something like, "It would be best if it was the Flipper 'cause otherwise this could cause lots of shit, you know."

"Do you think at this moment I really care about you or your fuckin' bikies or anything at all that you represent?" I snapped.

He was amazed that I was speaking to him in that tone, like he was nothing to me. All he did was represent a life my brother had been involved in, a life that had clearly let him down, one that my whole family hated. They had let my brother down in such a big way, and this fool was trying to make out he was there because he cared about James. I don't think so.

Arsehole Maria was standing there with her arms folded, sobbing. I didn't care about her at all. To me, she was with the enemy, so she was like him. She somehow was responsible, I just didn't know how. I had been very suspicious of her for a long time, and here she was with this clown. I didn't know how to handle her as being a woman of power. I would have to be careful what I said to her. She knew a lot of criminals.

By now, I was starting to get really upset, as I just wanted to see my brother. I would have to deal with the Maria thing later. I approached the front desk. I asked, "Please, I won't touch anything. I just need to see him. I need to be sure."

He looked at me and said, "It is James, and I'm really sorry, but you can't see him yet. Forensics needs to take samples from him, and he is a real mess. It would only upset you more. You will be able to see him in a couple of days."

I sobbed and just stood there in such pain. I asked them, "How do I explain to my mum? How do I tell her that I wasn't allowed to see him?" I just couldn't breathe again. My chest was so tight, I nearly fainted. One's body can only take so much stress. They asked me to sit down and take a few deep breaths, and I tried desperately to gain composure. I put my head into my hands. I just let out this almighty cry, like it had come from the very depths of my soul. It was like a pain that you can't heal, a pain so intense that there was nothing anyone could do.

People were staring at me. I was losing my grip that I had tried so hard to hold on to. There was no help. I was lost in my own thoughts, where no one else could be. No one could hurt me, as I was so numb I couldn't feel anything anyway. My breathing was settling down as I lifted my head. I felt really dizzy and sick.

Richard was standing there talking on the phone. Arron was just watching all of us. Richard got off the phone and approached us, saying, "We need to take Jenny and go to Frankino's house. This is our best chance to get him if he is responsible for this." Tony would not have realized that Jenny knew where he lived, but James had taken her there without his knowledge. So the police might be able to catch him red-handed.

Sambo was trying to make small talk. I wasn't interested in anything he had to say. It was probably the bikies themselves who got Tony to kill James. I had terrible things coming into my head. I wanted to blame someone so badly. I believe that we all have the right to an opinion; maybe it's not true, maybe it is.

The police took Jenny with them. I told her I would see her later. Maria was not impressed by me talking to Jenny. She asked me again why Jenny was here. "She has known James since we were kids, for God's sake," I told her. James had been involved with three business with Jenny and was always around, and this real smart lawyer didn't know why? Hmm. *You are just a bitch*, I was thinking. *You fucked James over. I just don't know how far you have gone.*

My cousin and I decided to leave, as there was no way they were going to let me see James. We went outside. There were reporters everywhere, cameras flashing, people yelling at me, trying to shove the microphone in my face. My cousin just sheltered me so we could get through them.

The drive home was so long. We stopped at my counsellor's on the way back to my mum's. I walked in and Gay just happened to be at the front. I was so upset, she grabbed me and gave me a hug. I was beside myself with emotions that I had never dealt with. My breathing was erratic; my heart was racing. It was as though my whole physical existence was in overdrive. Gay just held me and waited for me to catch my breath. The words I screamed out were, "James … James … James is dead!" I wept and sobbed in her arms as we walked into her office.

I sat there with no expression on my face. It was though my spirit had been drained from my body. My whole life with my brother was making my head spin. I had no words to say; the pain was so intense.

Gay spoke to me in a calming voice, not offering any advice, just encouraging me to talk it out. I sat there for a while. I knew eventually I had to drive back to Mum's. We talked for a while, and it gave me time to clear my head.

Eventually I decided it was time to go to Mum's. Jenny was with the police, and I estimated she would be with them for some time. As we left Gay's, I just wanted to escape, but there was nowhere to run. My kids needed me, and I needed them to make me understand that life would still go on. My mum needed me more; I just couldn't deal with her pain. I had nothing to offer her, as I was struggling myself.

When we arrived at Mum's, there were cars and people everywhere. The newspeople were out in front of the house. As we walked in, it was overwhelming. Mum said the police had just left. They had come to tell her that her son, James, had been killed. They were only four hours too late.

People were speaking to me. It was like they were talking in a different language. I could hear them, but none of it made any sense. My mother was so distraught. My younger sister was trying to comfort her the best way she could. We all just sat there trying to make sense of it all.

Jenny returned. She had taken the police to where Tony was living and had told them about the fight James had with him. The TV people had been waiting for a while now and asked if we would give an interview. They were all parked out in front of Mum's house. Why would people want to see someone in so much pain? We talked about it and decided that we would all do it. We sat down and did the interview, but out of all that was said, they only aired what suited them.

I left my mum's with my cousin. We decided I needed some serious brain-numbing. What could do that? On my way back, I stopped at Natalie's to see if the children were okay. The eldest one asked if he could come with me. Natalie said it would be okay so he could see my mum. Having the eldest one there meant a great deal to Mum. She had lost her only son, and the prospect of losing two grandchildren was the furthest thing from her mind. That cruel event would happen in the coming days.

The day seemed to never end. I decided at some point it was time to go home. Jenny asked to come back to my place; she seemed kind of lost. Her whole world had been ripped apart like ours. Without any warning, she was standing in a spot she had never been in before. It is a black hole you really can't see the end of.

I remember the first night; it was so awful. All I wanted to do was scream and cry and try to get my head around what was going on. The police rang me in the early evening and told me they had a suspect. I knew it was Tony. They said they would ring me later and were hoping to lay charges. I was so numb it really didn't make a huge difference. James was gone, and we couldn't bring him back.

I sat there getting a bit drunk. The phone rang about ten o'clock. They had charged Tony Frankino with the wilful murder of my brother. As much as it was a relief, it didn't stop the pain. There were still so many unanswered questions. It was like the police had put their input in, but we still had nothing.

The next couple of days rolled along with the phone constantly ringing and people trying to help and trying to make some sense out of it. I floundered; I really can't remember what I did or was doing for great parts of those days.

Friday came, and we were supposed to be organizing James's funeral, even though we had no idea what was to be done. I was going in to identify James. The police were waiting for forensics to be finished with James's body. It seemed like forever. It was probably the hardest blow, other than actually losing James, as there was no reality until we saw the body. Finally the phone rang and it was Richard telling me that we could go and identify James today. Identify my brother. My mind was still numb. I didn't know what to expect. All these thoughts were racing around in my head as I tried to focus on what I was about to do. I really had no idea.

Richard said Maria was also going to be there. I still don't know why she bothered. Jenny came too, and we went to the hospital to meet the police at the morgue. We arrived totally bewildered and unaware of what was about to happen. The police escorted us in, and there on the lounge was Maria and that fuckin' Sambo. Not him again. *What is going on?* My instincts told me this was wrong. I walked over to them both and said, "What the fuck are you doing here?" She mumbled something to me, but I did not hear what she said. Maybe I was being a bit hard on her, I don't know. Maybe she really did love and care about my brother.

Sambo said, "Let's all try to get along."

I asked him again, "What are you doing here? What, did you have to make sure it is James?" I screamed at him to fuck off. This was not where he should be. It was not his business. He had deserted my brother long ago. I kept yelling, "What, do you have to see your handiwork?"

Maria just sat there. When I looked at her, I could see that she was upset. Maybe not like us, but we all show emotion in different ways. At that point, I just became overwhelmed.

Richard said, "Clara, stop and think about what you are about to do." My heart sank. It was beating so hard, I thought it was going to jump out of my chest. My breathing was becoming rapid as he led me to the door. I stopped for a moment. I just froze. My thoughts were, *God, please let this be a mistake.*

Richard opened the door. He asked me if I wanted him to come in with me. I just shook my head. The tears were rolling down my face as I stepped into this cold room. My body was shaking. I walked over and stood there for a moment, just looking at the shape on this board, thinking, *Maybe this is a mistake. Maybe it's not really James.* As I walked slowly over to him, my breathing was short and my body was tense. I was shaking uncontrollably. He lay there like he was asleep, like he was at peace.

I walked closer, and now I could see his face. I looked at the outline of the features to be sure. He was so still. The rest of his body was covered, I guess because of all the damage that the bullets had done. I looked at him, touching his face, just wanting him to wake up, but he didn't. The tears were streaming down my face.

I was now standing right next to him. I screamed; I was wailing with pain. I started to shake him. "James, get up please, James!" I was so overwhelmed. I climbed onto him and just lay there. I wanted him to move, but he didn't. "Please, James, just wake up." I kept thinking, *What have they done to you? You did not deserve this.*

I was so emotional. Richard yelled out, "Do you want me to come in?" I sobbed back no. I just lay there with James, holding him, crying, not wanting to let him go. The more I stayed in there, the more surreal it seemed. James was my hero, and now he lay there dead as I lay across him. Our whole lives flashed in front of my eyes. Sobbing more now, I just didn't want to let him go. He felt so cold; it was like touching wax. *Hey, James, they had to shoot you. Real people stand and face their enemies. Cowards pull out guns.*

James was my protector, and now he was gone. I could hear Richard calling to me. I just didn't want to let James go. *They can't hurt you no more, James.* I remember kissing him on the forehead as my tears ran onto him. *Please, God, take good care of my little brother. He has suffered enough.*

I pulled myself up and hopped off of James. I sat there numb, thinking, *What now?* I walked to the door. Jenny was waiting to come in. I think my face said it all. The sadness is something you just can't hide, no matter how you try. Devastation is transparent.

After Jenny entered the room, I heard her wail a scream that went straight through me. I gather that's what they heard when I was in there. As I sat there, I couldn't believe they had sent a bikie to see if James was really dead. I couldn't help myself. I looked at Sambo and said, "Yeah, you're glad." He just looked back at me. I said, "You let him down, you and your club. *Brotherhood.* What fuckin brotherhood? You used him and then you didn't watch his back. You and the rest of them are as guilty as that psycho that's been charged."

Sambo said, "We aren't happy about this at all. You're wrong."

I screamed at him, "You are a liar. You let him down. You let this happen."

Richard came over and grabbed me, as at that point I was sobbing. I screeched at Maria, asking her what sort of person was she.

Jenny had been in there a while now. So Arron, the other policeman, knocked on the door, and Jenny came out. Maria and Sambo went in then. I was so disgusted that they had been allowed to go in. They weren't there for very long.

Richard had me sign James's identification paper. Richard had walked myself and Jenny out to the car park. Unfortunately, Maria had parked next to us. As Jenny and I stood there talking, we were both so upset. We were talking about Sambo being there. Maria and Sambo came out, and Sambo was just staring at us.

Maria approached her car. She stood there for a moment and then spoke to us. "Are you going to make the funeral arrangements today?"

I just glared at her.

"Why? asked Jenny.

"Because I think I should be able to be part of it," Maria said.

"Why?" asked Jenny.

"Because I was his partner."

"No you weren't," Jenny yelled. "I was and have been for twelve years. Haven't I, Clara?"

I thought, *I just can't do this today with these women.*

Maria said to Jenny, "What makes you more entitled to than me?"

Jenny replied, "He only used you."

"For what?" asked Maria.

"Think about it. You helped him with certain things. You helped him with money. He used you, you stupid bitch."

Maria started to get a bit teary. This was not right. Maybe she did have feelings. Maybe I just wanted to blame her as well.

She asked me what funeral people I was going to. I told her the lady ones near the clubhouse. She said to me, "I will meet you there."

"Whatever," I replied. I really did not care. I was so numb coming out of the morgue. I had to ring my mum to tell her it was James, so I really couldn't be bothered with all the fuss that these two women were making. I really didn't care. They all had been part of his life at some point. "You want to come? Come."

As we were driving to the funeral directors', Jenny was so angry about Maria coming. I told her not to worry.

We all descended on the funeral home. Poor people, they really didn't know what was about to hit them. In we all went.

A really nice lady came out. I explained that we were there to make funeral arrangements for my brother. She was really nice. She then went and got another lady—the lady who would deal with us. Her name was Shana.

Shana invited all of us into a room. We all sat down. The lady asked me about my brother and what sort of funeral would we like. I was just about to answer when Maria piped up, "You will be dealing with me."

"Oh," said the lady.

Then Jenny said, "No, you will be dealing with *me*."

The woman looked puzzled. "Mmm," she said. She looked at me to give her some indication of who she should be listening too. Next minute, they started to yell at each other. I was just sitting there bewildered. I couldn't believe they were carrying on again.

The lady calmed them down and again tried to talk about the funeral. Both women wanted the final say in what was going to happen. In the end, the woman said to me, "What does your family want?"

I was lost in thought. My brother was gone, and they were carrying on. *God*, I said, *if he wasn't dead, I would kill him myself for leaving this mess.* It was like a movie scene where women are fighting over a man. Well, we were living it.

The lady suggested we all have a bit of a say. Maria calmed down. Clearing her throat, she asked if James could have a plain coffin, but majestic; not too busy, but strong and sturdy like him. Shana looked at Jenny and myself and said, "Is this okay?" I was just so devastated, I did not answer.

Finally we agreed James would want something simple. We then agreed on the flower arrangement: we would have one big wreath full of red roses that would cover half his coffin. Whilst we were sitting there being polite, the woman kept asking me if I was okay. I kept shrugging. At this point, I was just allowing the two of them to sort it out.

We then went into what he would wear. Maria was hell-bent on putting James into a suit. We all knew that's not who he was. James wore casual clothes—flannel shirts, black jeans or even longish shorts, but a suit? No way.

Well, she kept saying that's what she wanted him buried in. Jenny was carrying on and saying, "No, that is not what he would want." To me, it did not really matter. He was gone, and I knew I would never see my brother again. In the end, we agreed to disagree. I just wanted it over with.

Next, the cars. Maria did not want to be with us nor us with her, so three cars were ordered. Next, the music. I got to choose most of the music. First there would be "From a Distance" by Bette Midler, a great song about peace. Next would be Eric Clapton's "Tears in Heaven," and then there would be "Wind beneath My Wings." Maria wanted a song whilst we were burying him: "Our Love Will Go On."

Pall-bearers had to be picked. I felt this was the family's choice, so we started to debate. It was a power struggle. Maria wanted bikies from the Devil's Dogs, but there was no way in hell I was going to let that happen. Another argument started.

I held my ground this time. "No," I said. "You can have two, no more."

She wanted three. She was persistent. She wanted Sambo, Milo, and Rhino.

"No way. Fuck Milo."

So she had her two in. We agreed, much to my disgust. I knew my brother would have turned in his grave. The others were cousins and one friend. It was done.

Maria said, "Who is going to organize the chapel?"

My brother was not Catholic but we all were, so I asked the priest at my children's school to do the funeral. He agreed. Maria was supposed to do the eulogy. That's what she wanted. Next, we had to decide on a day, as it was now nearly two weeks since James's death—a long time for a family to wait to bury a loved one.

Maria insisted that the funeral be on a Saturday, as she didn't want to take any more time off from her job. We agreed, even though we didn't want to. I just needed for this to be over. Then the arguing started again about their roles in his life. They both kept asking me questions I really wasn't going to answer.

The woman asked who was going to pay. As Maria was also my brother's partner, she said she would pay and then claim it against the estate. This never happened. My family paid for the funeral. Not one cent came from the estate. My brother's funeral was left to us.

We walked outside with them still carrying on. I'd had enough. "Let's go," I said to Jenny. We drove home in silence. I just did not want to hear anymore about the two of them. Thank God Natalie never got involved with it, or the other woman my brother was seeing, a nurse that he had been spending time with for a while. I really don't know how he did it. So many women, so many lies.

I was driving, all the while lost in thought. I had a little smile on my face and began shaking my head, talking to James in my mind. I was saying, *You knew this would be bad. Lucky you're not here. This is just a terrible mess.*

On arriving back at my mum's, I gave her the bit of paper that I had signed. It was just to identify James. At that point, we did not realize that we still had not been issued a death certificate. This was something that would not be issued for many years. I did not realise it took so long for the death certificate to come It had to go through the coroner and a full investigation on how my brother died Funny I though it obvious that he was shot too deathI wonder why the coroner had to signoff on it strange but Somewhere in my far mind I often thought that maybejust maybe He was still alive is this why we hadn't received the death certificate I often hoped that he was in some sort of under cover program and he was safe but Its funny how your heart will long for something so much you start to hope But then it comes the piece of paper you really do not want the final thing that tells me my brother is no more

My mum was so sad. The life had been drained from her soul. She was a woman broken. This was clearly someone in need of spiritual guidance. My mother had once believed heavily in the Church, but not for many years now. She had lost faith, but I think in these dark times it may have helped her. She kept asking me why her son was taken. Why did God take him? I said to her, "God did not take him. Someone else thought he had that right." At least in the moment of his death, he did not suffer long. Not that this was any relief at all, but maybe that's what got me through.

As the funeral got closer, there was no peace for our mum. She blamed herself completely, though it was not her fault at all.

I decided to bite the bullet and go and see Maria about letting my mum go to James's house. As I was driving to her home, all I could do was cry. What a terrible, terrible mess this had all become. With his death, problems with all these woman was just not fair. I felt like I couldn't mourn my brother, as they were constantly at me.

I arrived with a heavy heart. I knocked on her door, and she answered. "What do you want?"

I said, "I'm here to see if you would allow my mum the opportunity to go to James's house before anything is moved, just to let her be in the last place her son was."

She glared at me. "No. No way. Who do you think you are?"

I replied, "James's sister. His family."

She huffed and poked her chest out to me. I really wasn't in the mood for this. "You betrayed me," she screeched. "You should have told me about the other women."

I said, "It wasn't my job to tell you anything. He was my brother, and even though I didn't agree with his life choices, it wasn't up to me."

She screeched at me again.

I said, "Look, you reckon you knew my brother really well. You know if I had uttered a word to anyone, he would have ripped my tongue out and choked me with it. Why don't you go ask Sambo or Milo about Jenny? They all knew."

"Mmm," she said. "No to your request."

I was stunned. "Why? It's his mum!"

"She does not deserve to go there."

I said, "Who are you to make that judgement? Who do you think you are? He left you weeks ago. you told me yourself that you did not care about him."

"Mmm," she said again. "Well, he brought it all upon himself."

I said, "How can you say that?"

She replied, "He was told not to have anything to do with Tony."

I said, "Who told him that?"

She replied, "The club."

I said, "They have no right. He was not part of them anymore."

She grunted, "Do you really believe that you ever get out?"

"No," I said, "but there was always hope."

She glared at me. There were tears in her eyes, but whether from sorrow or just plain anger I do not know. I leaned against her wall. I hadn't eaten in days. My weight had plummeted. I was so weak. Arguing with her was pointless. I asked her again, "Please let my mum just go there. You can be there with her. She is a broken woman."

"So what?" she said. "She also brought this upon herself."

I was amazed how cruel and mean she could be. We argued about two cars at my brother's that I informed her I would get back. She said, "I promised them to the club."

I looked at her as I walked away and said, "Yeah, good luck with that."

On the way home, I felt such sadness for my mum. Even though I was blaming her, this was not right. She deserved to be allowed to go there.

I got back and told my mum what Maria had said. Mum was gutted, but she said to me she did not expect anything other than that from Maria.

The next day, the day before the funeral, I received a call from Maria. "I'm not going to write the eulogy. You can do it." I just hung up the phone. This woman was a thorn in my side. How she could blame me? I really couldn't understand. This mess I knew was just going to get worse.

It did indeed get worse. Let me pause here to tell the story of those two cars, so you can understand how Maria operated and what I had to deal with as the one caught between her and Jenny.

After my brother was murdered and the reality had set in, there were things that needed sorting out, including two cars that were at his house that belonged to me. James had rebuilt a Camaro that he had brought in from the states in 1992. He was spending money like it was never going to run out. He needed money to pay for the car and started to fix it. I was pretty flush at the time, so I loaned him the money, but there was always a *but* with my brother. I told him I wanted the car put into my name until such time as he paid me back.

Well, time was ticking on. James borrowed more money from me to keep fixing the car. No one knew about our arrangement; that was the way my brother wanted it. The Camaro was licensed, and James kept it at his house. The car was put into my name, so at least I had some sort of reassurance that one day I would be paid back.

Time kept marching on. James bought many cars and sold them. He bought an old Holden from a guy down in a small country town. It was a wreck. James bought it anyway. He borrowed more money from me, again with the promise that one day we would sell the cars and make money. *Yeah, right*, I thought. But I kept on giving him money, hoping that the cars would make us a profit.

After my brother's murder, things changed very quickly. Unbeknown to me, James had gotten someone to forge my signature on the Camaro papers and put it in his name, as he needed security against his coffee shop. So when I asked Maria for the car, I received an abrupt answer of, "No, go to hell."

I took matters into my own hands. I went to my brother's property where he had been living before his death. Myself, Jenny, and another person by the name of Ricky drove into my brother's driveway. Maria was unaware that Jenny had keys to the property, as James had many different lives, each one not knowing about the other.

Jenny opened the front door and, to our horror, my brother's home was a terrible mess. There were things scattered all over the place. Someone had obviously been looking for something. I was taken aback. How could she do this to his stuff? How could she be so vindictive? I walked around in horror, finally sitting down to catch my breath.

Jenny started to cry. "This is not how he lived. Why did she do this?" I had no answer. This had gone beyond a women's squabble. As I gained composure, I was glad my mum had not come; it would have been devastating to her. I walked outside, and my two cars were there, but some of my brother's other vehicles were missing. I really did not have any idea where they could be.

I made a decision to call a tow company. I would remove my two cars. I had the keys to both of them, but the batteries were flat. The tow-truck drivers arrived, and I asked them two load both the Camaro and the old Holden. I remembered Maria telling me she had promised these cars to the bikies. *Over my dead body*, I thought.

The tow-truck drivers started to get organized. Jenny asked me, "Do you think I should take some of James's things?"

I really did not know the answer. "Do what you think is right," I said. James's death was still haunting me. I could not think clearly; I could not focus. I felt sick in the pit of my gut as my cars were loaded. I then said to the tow-truck drivers, "Take the trailer as well." It had a couple of my brother's go-carts in it.

Jenny and Ricky were putting small things into the cars as we left the property. I felt such a sense of loss. He was gone, and he was not coming back. He was dead. It hit me, and I fell to pieces. I came home, locked everything away, and just cried. I would never see him again. I would never look at him. My brother was dead. It was at that point I came to realize just how much pain I was in. My other half was gone. He was all of me.

The very next week, I had a phone call from the detective in charge of my brother's murder investigation. He said Maria had reported that James's house had been broken into. I said, "I don't know what you're talking about."

He asked me, "Do you have the two cars?"

I replied, "Yes, they are mine."

He said to me, "Did you break in?"

I said, "No, Jenny had keys to the property."

He said Maria wanted the cars back. I said, "Guess what? Maria can go fuck herself. They belong to me."

He said, "There are other ways to deal with this."

I replied, "I know, but I do not care."

After a couple of weeks, a meeting was called between myself, Maria, and the detective at a small bar next to the police department in town. Maria was being her normal self, trying to bully me. I would not succumb. I would not be bullied or intimidated by anyone. I had survived more than she could ever handle.

We made an agreement, not that I wanted to. It was agreed that all of the things that Jenny had removed would be returned. As much as I did not think this was right, I had nothing to back up Jenny's claim to my brother's personal stuff—but I did have claims to both cars.

As the months went by, more and more pressure was put on me about the cars. I made a decision to give the cars to the state and then fight for them. I gave the old Holden up first. Then I sat down for hours every night finding paperwork that linked me to the Holden. I found documents all the way back to when it was purchased. I took my case to the civil court. I was up against the state of Western Australia, Natalie, and Maria. Ironically, they had joined forces. I believe it was to both of their advantages, and for no other reason than I could not afford a lawyer. So there I was—I was David, going up against Goliath.

A court date approached. I was pumped; I was ready. On the day of the hearing, neither Natalie nor Maria appeared. It was left to the state and me to fight it out. I was brilliant. I put my case forward with all of my documents. The judge took a break, and after about two hours he came back and awarded me the car. He ordered it returned, and he ordered that Natalie, being the administrator of my brother's trust, should pay the costs. I was so excited. I had won! The next thing was to return the Camaro and fight for that. I was on a high. I knew my brother was with me all the way.

I rang the detective again, and I said, "Come get the Camaro. Let's do this."

Another court case came around six months later—the same judge, the same set of circumstances. No one but me turned up. Again I presented my case. It was at this time that the judge made an unusual statement. He said to the lawyer for the other side, "I need time to read through these documents."

I piped up and said, "All due respect, your honour, one would presume that you would have done that already."

He was not impressed, so we went away for a couple of hours. On our return, the judge looked puzzled. He said to the state lawyer, "I really do not know what to do here."

I piped up again and said, "Excuse me, your honour, one would presume that you'd do what you did last time and give me back my car."

The judge asked the state lawyer if he had any problem with that. The lawyer said, "No sir, it seems the other parties are really just wasting our time. They have had their chance and did not come. So no, your honour, I have no problem."

I felt this amazing feeling like, *Wow, I took on the law and I won*. Well, civil cases are a bit different. The judge awarded me my car back. I knew that I would win. I knew I was right. I was not afraid. The people who had made it so very difficult for me had no case anyway; they just thought that I would melt under pressure. They were wrong.

Back to the funeral preparations. After Maria called to say she wouldn't do the eulogy, I sat down and thought, *I've got one day to do this*. I had waited many days before putting his death notice in the paper. The words for that were hard enough. I struggled, because although I knew what it was like to lose a family member, it had never been anyone this close before, no one who was ripped out of my life. There had been no warning, no goodbyes, no one to be with him in his final moment.

I was asked once, if I could, would I have changed his death? No, I replied, because it is apparent that it was inevitable. But I would have liked for us to be there in his final moments, to be able to comfort him, to hold his hand as he slipped away, to just be there is all I think we would have wanted. We were robbed of that time. The person who shot my brother took that moment away.

This was my death notice:

Jobson, James (Big Jim)

I have no words to describe a pain that I have never felt. A grief so overwhelming that I feel nothing else. A lifetime of memories is what I have. They have taken your body but not your soul, for that lives inside of the people that loved you the most. I will miss you for the rest of my life. You were a son, you were a partner, you were a father, but most of all you were my brother. I will always be proud and honoured to have shared your life. You will always be my JIMMY BIGSHOT. Rest in peace now. All the pain has gone.

This was not easy, but I managed to get it done. Now, on to the eulogy. Hours went by. Finally, I just wrote it. It flowed out of me. This was my version, no one else's. I don't think anyone else could have managed it. One of my brother's friends—another girl, by the way, but she really was just his friend—actually wrote a farewell to him herself. I thought she showed courage, as her boyfriend was a Satan's Sons member.

The morning of the funeral was hell. The media had been hounding our family and just loving all the crap that was going on. Maria had decided that she would get her own way at the funeral. She phoned to inform me she did not want to be near Jenny.

At this point, we had not had any contact with my brother's children. That had been stopped, for some reason. Natalie had now joined in the bitch-fighting. Maria got Natalie on her side. God knows why Natalie even bothered, considering it was Maria my brother had left her for.

Jenny was at her home one day when she heard all this screaming out front. Not knowing what was going on, she went outside There were Maria and Natalie in her driveway. You see, Jenny lived in one of my brother's houses, and Maria and Natalie were yelling terrible things at Jenny, telling her to get out of the house, evicting her. They were threatening to both beat her up.

Jenny just screeched back at them, telling them to fuck off. Meanwhile, Jenny's daughter rang the police. By the time the police came, Maria and Natalie had taken off. The police took a statement from Jenny, and they went and spoke to Maria and Natalie about the incident. Nothing came of it.

The police came to the funeral just to make sure there was no trouble. A bit late, really. Where were they before?

The long trip to the cemetery was silent as we all gathered our thoughts, finding strength just to make it through the day. On arriving, I saw the bikies. I hated the fact that they were going to be any part of this. It was them, I was sure, who had organized this horrible thing. But I just got out of the car and stood there. I felt bewildered, like I was lost in some sort of time warp. I felt totally alone. People were talking to me, but there was no sense in what they were saying. It seemed so unreal.

My mum was helped by relatives. I still had a stick up my arse. I think back and realize what an arsehole I was.

Sambo approached me and asked where Maria was. I just glared at him and said, "I don't know, and I don't care."

As the people gathered, one of my cousins stood with me, saying random things. She also had lost a brother through terrible circumstances many years before, so in a way she understood the terrible pain that I was in.

As everyone gathered, the pall-bearers took their places. I saw out of the corner of my eye Maria with my brother's eldest child. I was really drained. As the presentation started, I was looking at my mum. It was the saddest thing I have ever seen in my whole life. We all waited, and then it started—the long walk to the chapel.

I was overwhelmed. I just felt nothing; the pain was too intense. We had asked people not to bring flowers or wreaths, as the large one we had on top of his coffin was enough and we wanted to keep it simple. But I couldn't help myself. I brought a small bundle of flowers and placed them inside the hearse. Mum had put roses from her house on his coffin, as she felt it was more personal. They were something she had grown.

As we arrived at the chapel, the first song started playing. I noticed that there were some bikies from rival clubs there. James had friends from those clubs. I was amazed they were there, but the ones who were looked clearly shaken, and I could see they were truly my brother's friends.

In the chapel, time stood still. The priest was talking about James and doing whatever priests do. I truly cannot remember what he was saying. It was like a silent movie. The next song came on, "Tears in Heaven," and after that, the priest called me up to read my eulogy. I stood up feeling very unsure of myself and walked to the microphone. Standing there for a moment, I found a strength that I had not felt for a while. I felt James was with me, making me strong enough to get through these next few minutes. Looking out into the crowd, I could see people's faces and hear tears and sobs coming from all over the place. A friend had come up to support me—just in case I fainted, I suppose.

"I stand before you today a sister in so much pain that there are no words to describe it," I began. "A member of a family filled with disbelief and despair. We are here today to celebrate the life of my brother, James Jobson. He was a son to Josey and Alfred. a brother to myself and Sabrina, a father and an uncle, a relative to many, a friend to few, a mate to everyone. To know him was to love him. He was as strong as ten men and had courage to match a lion. A heart so wanting to have a better life. It's the strength and courage I draw from my brother that has kept me going.

"A childhood filled with many memories, some we wish to remember and some we wish to forget. As children, we spent a considerable amount of time together. We would play cowboys and Indians. We would watch wrestling and practice the moves during commercials. A lover of baked beans and a good Chinese meal. A troubled teenager, you came to enjoy rugby, motorbikes, and fast cars. Rebuilding your first car was quite an achievement. A bouncer you became, and a shareholder in Telstra. Most of us who knew you well would agree, James loved the phone, always calling someone to have a chat. The gym had now become a big part of your life. And your first Harley was a dream come true. But through these years, two things occurred. You met your children's mum and joined a club. Your troubled childhood had now taken over. A need to belong sent James on the road he chose to live. Being part of a club was being in a brotherhood that in the end let him down.

"So now, one of the greatest things in my brother's life was his first child. Fatherhood was a challenge in itself, as having no role model, James found this adjustment hard, but the love he had for his child was enough to make James receive help, for he wanted so badly to be a better person. Then James's second child was born, and James decided that with his two children was where he wanted to be. So now a new road, a father who loved his two children more than life itself. Every moment that James could spend with them, he cherished. He was proud and honoured these two little men were in his life. And now I'm sure he will guide them in spirit for the rest of their lives.

"A need to change was also a great challenge for James. He worked so hard at becoming a better person. For this itself tried his very soul. Slowly chipping away, he pushed forward to be halfway there and then was robbed at the finish. It's so unfair. But the lessons in our lives that make us better people are the ones hardest to learn. My brother was so strong in character. To have him roar at you sent shivers down your spine. To see him cry was to know he was human. James wore many hats in his life, but the one hat for me is that he was my brother. I am proud and honoured to have shared this extraordinary life of a man who I will truly miss for the rest of my life. Rest in peace."

This was so hard. I just could not read his friend's poem, so I handed it to the priest. It was as follow:

> *James*
> Your friendship meant the world to me
> And I just want you to know
> I'll always feel close to you
> Wherever you may go
> I just can't help wonder
> What life would be like today
> If you and I had never met
> And we simply gone another way
> When I think of all the occasions
> When you been there to see me through
> It makes me wonder how on earth
> Am I going to manage without you
> Because friendship is a precious gift
> And I know my whole life through
> I'll always be so grateful
> That I had a friend like you
> So I'll always feel so lucky
> That the paths we chose that day
> Led us to each other
> And not some other way
> SLEEP PEACEFULLY MY FRIEND
> —*Angela*

The last song came on as we all stood and left the church to do the final walk. Rest in peace, my brother. If tears could build a stairway and memories a lane, I'd walk right up to heaven to bring you home again.

> *Who are you to judge the life I live?*
> *I know I am not perfect, and I don't live to be.*
> *But before you start pointing fingers, make sure your hands are clean.*
> —*Bob Marley*

# CHAPTER 8

# *The Trial*

Tony Frankino was charged with the wilful murder of my brother, James Jobson. The police called and said he would remain in custody and that he would be making a brief court appearance. I was relieved and not surprised a bit by the charge or the person. This is the story that came out of how the murder was committed.

It was four forty-five a.m. My brother was sitting outside the gym, waiting for it to open. James went there every day to work out. He found it a way of relieving stress. The streetlights flickered as he sat in the cool air. The manager of the gym was upstairs getting ready for the day; knowing James would be out in front, he always opened a bit early. James was sitting on the bench outside, flicking through the newspaper, thinking today was no different from any other day.

James heard a noise coming from the garden and looked up to see what it was. Standing in front of him was a man dressed in dark clothes wearing a motorbike helmet. The man pointed a gun at my brother. Realizing this was serious, James jumped up. *Bang!* The first shot was fired. It went through James's arm. As James desperately tried to get away, *bang*! The second bullet went through James's side. The manager heard the shots and panicked. People in nearby houses were awakened by the noise.

James ran towards the gym door, but it was locked. James was banging on the glass, the gunman now behind him. The manager was still hiding upstairs. A cleaner who was inside also was scared. James kept on smashing at the door, and eventually it shattered. James ran in and the gunman followed him. Although James had blood pouring out of his arm and side, he scampered into the building. The gunman then fired again, this time into James's back. James went to his knees, and then the gunman again fired into James's back. The manager had come down, and the gunman pointed the gun at him and pulled the trigger. Luckily for him, there were no more bullets.

The manager stood there in complete shock. What could he do? James was lying on the ground covered in blood, trying desperately to breathe. His breaths were getting shorter. It was getting harder. The manager tried to help but did not know what to do.

The gunman ran from the building, got on his motorbike, and sped off. The manager rang the police and ambulance. A security guard who was in the area had heard the gunshots and came as soon as he could. He tried to stop the bleeding. He ran out to get his first-aid bag, stumbling a bit, as he was scared that the gunman was going to return. He finally got his bag and returned to James. The manager was there as well.

The guard heard James say, "They got me!" James told the guard he did not want to die, that he had two children. The guard asked James if he knew who shot him. James was in so much pain. All his internal organs had been damaged. He was struggling to breath, gasping for air. He was starting to fade.

The security guard again asked him, "Who shot you?"

James said, "Tony Franki …" Well, that is what the security guard recalls. The guard kept talking to James, trying to reassure him that he was going to be okay. James kept saying, "I don't want to die."

The ambulance arrived, and masses of police. They put James on a trolley and into the ambulance. People all over the neighbourhood had awakened to this tragedy. This was a quiet city, not the Middle East. People should not be killed in the streets.

Maria arrived before seven; I'm not really sure how she found out. I asked her once, and she replied that she had been listening to a police scanner and decided to check it out. Well, that's what she said.

The ambulance pulled away, lights flashing, sirens blaring. At the hospital, James was declared dead on arrival. He had lost his fight. No amount of inner strength could get him through. The shooter made sure there would be no hope.

The police were everywhere, knocking on doors, trying desperately to piece together what had happened. They interviewed the manager and the security guard about the shooting. The guard told them what James had said. He said he asked James who shot him and gave the police the name. It baffled the police; searching through their data, they could find no Tony Franki anywhere. Police were now combing nearby houses and streets for witnesses. They were looking for the motorbike and gun.

Meanwhile, we were at the hospital. When Jenny and I were talking to the police officers and told them about the fight James had with Tony, I thought it was odd that they asked how we knew that last name. We walked away to discuss what we should tell the police. Jenny was a bit hesitant, as Sambo was eyeballing us the whole time, desperately trying to listen to our conversation and intimidate us.

That day, police set up surveillance on Tony's house. They sat there for hours just watching to see if he made a move. After many hours, he emerged from the house and was seen loading a few large plastic rubbish bags into his car. The police waited and then followed him. He drove around the block a few times, I suppose to see if he was being followed. When he was satisfied that he wasn't, he proceeded to the dump.

The police, still on his tail, watched him pull into the dump, look around, and pull out the black plastic bags one at a time, looking around the whole time. In the bags he had put dark clothing—pants, shirt, and gloves with gunshot residue on them—and four cartridges that matched a .357 magnum, the same as the ones that killed my brother. Also in the bags was a motorbike helmet that matched what the manager had seen.

Tony was arrested and taken to the police station, where he was interviewed for a number of hours and eventually charged with the wilful murder of my brother, James Jobson, his best friend. He made a brief appearance in court and was remanded into custody to a later date. The police were now searching his house, where they found a small hydroponic set-up with a number of marijuana plants and a small amount of money. As they were searching Tony's house, they found that he had written to underworld figure Rocco Angolli. They also found hate notes written to my brother.

A day before the murder, Tony had placed a note on my brother's car suggesting to James that he was sorry for the fight they had. I believe it was a ploy to make my brother think it was all okay. My brother was murdered in what is described as a gangland-style killing. The papers just kept on printing terrible things about my brother. It was so cruel. No matter what you have done in your life, no one deserves to be gunned down in such a cowardly way. People who use guns in this way have no courage. They have no backbone. They are lower than pond scum.

As the months went by, Tony appeared in court on a regular basis. The legal system can sometimes drag on for months. Jenny and I were always in court on the days he made his brief appearances. I felt ill looking at him. He was someone I wished would just die. At one of his court appearances, Jenny and I were a metre away from him. I wanted to reach out and punch him.

When his name was called, he stood up. The judge read out the charges and asked if Tony Frankino was his name. The fool just mumbled. The judge asked if he knew and understood why he was in court. He replied no. It was at that moment I lost control. I stood up and yelled at him, "You dumb prick, you're here because you killed my brother!" I started to get very upset.

Richard charged in, picked me up, and carried me from the court. I was sobbing uncontrollably. I couldn't breathe. What is it with this man? Is he just a real big flipper, as the bikies had described him? Or was it that his mental-health problem did not let him face reality? I have never hated someone so much in my life. He infuriated me so much that day, I decided I would only go to the trial.

Tony had employed Justin Knight as his lawyer. As fate would have it, Knight was charged a number of years later with the murder of his wife, Lisa Knight. There were whispers around town about all sorts of evilness, but none were ever presented in court or could be proved. He would be acquitted and walk free. The family of his wife believed that he was the killer. Talk about justice going wrong. Law but no justice.

With every moment, we were getting closer to trial. My whole family was hoping for justice. My brother was a lot of things, but he did not deserve to die the way he did. The judge was Justice Judith Graw. The prosecutor was a man called Worthington, a smallish man, a little plump, who talked like he had a plum in his mouth. I never really liked him. I just did not get a good feeling about him He had been the prosecutor on my brother's bashing case, so I'm not really sure he tried his best. We were supposed to have a different prosecutor, but he was due to go on leave.

There were a number of police officers giving evidence. The police had witnesses from nearby houses, the manager of the gym, the security guard, forensic evidence—the list went on and on. The trial was set to go on for a number of weeks, and even though I did attend most days, I still had to go to work. My mum was there every day. She never missed one witness's evidence.

As both sides gave their opening speeches, it was evident from the start that Tony's lawyer, Justin Knight, would play on my brother's past in an attempt to raise reasonable doubt. My mum got so distressed listening to the evidence. I was just confused. All these witnesses with different accounts of the sound of bullets and the make of the motorbike. There was even a witness who gave a description. I don't know about you, but how on earth could you make a positive description when it's not even five o'clock in the morning? The Leisure Centre was not lit up well. The streetlights were a distance away, and the witness was eight hundred metres away. There was a slight haze and shadows. That witness must have awesome eyesight.

Every witness just wound up making the case for Tony. There were witnesses who said there were two motorbikes, others one. There was the sound of the bikes, again all different. Describing the sounds of the bullets was even worse. The conflicting testimony just went on and on.

The manager from the gym testified that he was inside when he heard loud noises. He realized that the noises came from where my brother was sitting. As he looked outside, he saw a person dressed in dark clothing wearing a dark helmet standing about five metres from my brother. He said he saw my brother barge at the door and ram it. The jury was shown video surveillance footage of my brother smashing the glass to get away from the gunman, and of the gunman following my brother in. The manager said he tried to make an 000 call. By the time he came to where my brother was, the security guard was there. He recalled that James was in a lot of pain, and there was blood everywhere. The security guard was talking to my brother.

The security guard, was called to give evidence. He described the scene as terrifying. He assisted my brother, trying desperately to stop the bleeding. All the while, he and the manager were in fear of their lives. The gunman had pointed a gun at the manager, and there was no telling if the gunman was going to come back. Both men were courageous in their efforts to help my brother.

The forensic evidence was long and boring. One of the forensic experts testified that the cartridges that Tony was found dumping at the dump were exactly the same as the ones that killed my brother. His gloves and hands tested positive for gunshot residue. His motorbike had gunshot residue on it. The clothing that he tried to dump had gunshot residue on it. The helmet that he threw out matched the manager's description.

The jury was also told that Tony owned a .357 Magnum, the same gun that killed my brother. He said it had been stolen from his vehicle a month before, but the theft was never reported to the police. Tony was an excellent shooter.

The doctor who did the autopsy on my brother gave a graphic description, saying the shooter knew where to fire the bullets so that every major organ was damaged. The doctor explained that my brother would have been in extreme pain, with his adrenaline racing, so the blood would have been pouring out of his body. The police who arrested Tony also gave evidence, saying that they caught him trying to dispose of all the objects.

But Justin Knight's argument was only about my brother's past links to bikies. Interesting, I think, as the jury never got to hear of Tony's history. My brother could not defend himself. All the while the papers were writing terrible things, like "Jobson was a traitor" or "Jobson was a turncoat." On and on they trashed him.

Tony said that he and my brother had never really had a falling out. He testified to what great friends they were. I believe he was like a volcano, just waiting to erupt and spew havoc on my brother's life. Tony was jealous of my brother, as James had been accepted into the bikie world, not only by one club but by two. Tony, on the other hand, was a joke. They all hated him because he was a threat, a very unstable person. No one feared him; it was his mental state that was sometimes the concern.

Tony testified that my brother had a falling out with some of the hierarchy of the Devil's Dogs gang and was trying to make his way back in. He said that James was going to make contact with Rocco Angolli, currently serving time in prison for trafficking drugs and jumping bail. Angolli had a few years earlier been beaten by the Devil's Dogs after a drug deal went bad. He told everyone that the Devil's Dogs were no good, and they were dogs themselves. The bashing took place at a restaurant where Angolli was beaten and brutalized, something I'm sure he never forgot.

Tony gave evidence suggesting my brother was to make contact with Angolli via the computer. What a laugh. My brother would not even have known how to turn on a computer, let alone work one. The phone was James's only source of information.

Then Tony changed his story and produced handwritten notes to Angolli. None were ever matched by a handwriting expert. No one ever suggested that it should be matched to my brother's writing. Both sides just let it go. Tony could have written them himself, who knows. The hypothesis was never tested. The jury was told that my brother James wanted to know if Angolli had put a price on the head of the bikies in question. They were Milo, Sambo, and two other members.

Tony testified that it was rumoured that these particular bikies had beaten Angolli, and he supposedly had put a hit out on them. Quite interesting that these particular men were also connected to the beating by Tony himself. Tony testified that James wanted the information to give to the bikies in order to gain their trust again.

Tony was allowed to produce a paper clipping about a street fight he'd had with the Mafia. The jury had no information about criminal records, medical records, or anything else about Tony; all the jury was told was how bad a man my brother was because he had been part of two bikie gangs.

The jury could have been told that Tony was in love with my brother and was jealous of his life. They were never told of the savage beating that Tony had received at the hands of senior Devil's Dogs because of the supposed rape of one of the bikie's girlfriends. The jury only heard that James was a dead man walking.

Prosecutor Worthington explained that James himself had identified his killer with his dying breath, telling the security guard "Tony Franki ...." Did the jury take into consideration he was dying, gasping for breath, in pain, that it would have been excruciating, with blood everywhere, just to say that much? Could the security guard have heard it wrong? Remember, he was scared that the killer was coming back. Could James have taken a breath when saying the last name? Did the jury ever consider how James was feeling? Could they really ever put themselves in that position?

"Beyond a reasonable doubt." That's all it took.

The trial went for three weeks. Every day was a terrible burden for my family. After a day and a half of deliberation, the judge discharged the jury when they could not reach a verdict on a wilful murder charge against Tony Frankino. He was remanded into custody until a status conference in November so new dates for a retrial could be set.

The retrial came around in 2007. Tony was now being represented by a Mr. Jackson, Justin Knight being busy with things happening in his own life. Mr. Jackson argued this time that the wrong man was on trial. He used the line that there were many possibilities. Mr. Jackson told the jury this was not the act of one man but of a group of people, and it was those people who should be on trial. "They think they are law unto themselves," Mr. Jackson kept on insisting.

The trial was before Justice Livingston. After all the witnesses and forensic evidence had been presented by the prosecution, Justice Livingston dismissed the case against Tony and said there was no case to answer. He believed there were a number of possibilities. Peter Jetson, the director of public prosecutions, was shocked that the judge would dismiss the case in that way. It was a very unusual decision, but the judge was entitled to make it. Jetson then met with prosecution lawyers to work through the evidence and find a basis for another appeal by the state.

Outside court, Tony broke down in tears, claiming that he was in fact the wrong man on trial and a lifelong friend of James Jobson. He said he would like an opportunity to speak to the family of his murdered friend. The newspaper asked me for a statement. I replied that my family was devastated and truly believed the decision was a miscarriage of justice. There were no words to describe a pain that could never heal.

Tony was now free to leave the country. As the prosecution worked endlessly for proof, the DPP took the case to the court of appeals and won the right to a third trial in the Supreme Court. He would not have been able to appeal a "not guilty" verdict but could appeal a dismissal made at the discretion of a judge.

The three court of appeals judges made a swift decision, saying that they would give their reason in writing, but Chief Justice Wally Mountreed made it quite clear that Justice Livingston had failed to follow accepted legal principles and take the prosecution case at its highest. He also said in his statement that it was not the function of a trial judge to form a view as to which of two versions was to be preferred. Justice Livingston seemed to have taken the slant most favourable to the accused on every piece of evidence. The appeals judges agreed it was the job of the jury to decide a person's guilt or innocence. All three judges agreed that Livingston's decision should be set aside.

Tony Frankino was not in court. His lawyer and his family had tried many times to contact him with no success. The federal police flew to Hong Kong to order his return. After several months, he handed himself in. He was in Hong Kong awaiting extradition. I was asked by the papers what our family thought of the news of a third trial. I said, "'The wheels of justice turn slowly,' and in this case they certainly have."

Finally, we had a date; a new judge, Justice Johnson; and a new jury. Could we be lucky this third time? One would have to ask, if what the defence had repeatedly used as the key to its argument—that there were other possibilities—was true, why would the DPP make another attempt to get this man found guilty of the murder? Another trial meant more publicity for my family. Would justice finally be done?

It was like *Groundhog Day*. All the witnesses came back again. All the experts gave their evidence again. After a few weeks, the jury was directed by the judge to make a decision. It seemed like forever, but when all you have is time, you think about what the jury had been allowed to hear. They heard nothing of Tony's past, only my brother's. Why couldn't we have told them the story about the really bad bashing and given them a motive for murder? Just maybe, with that, my brother's killer might be behind bars. But it seemed it wasn't going to go our way.

The jury came back again and told the judge they could not reach a verdict. The judge was not happy with that situation; she ordered the jury to go back out and reach one. I knew then it would not go our way. But at least I knew again that there were people on two juries who thought Tony killed my brother.

It was not long, and we were called back. A decision had been made. As the foreman of the jury told the judge that they had reached a verdict, I went totally numb, like my body was there but my soul was not. As I heard the "not guilty" verdict, I was shattered. My mum was a broken woman who could not be comforted. Was this our justice system? I did not want to hear any more. I walked outside. I was devastated.

All I could think of was how unfair it was that my brother who was murdered was actually the one on trial. The defence team had gone about destroying my brother. I do not know how defence lawyers sleep when they know that their clients are guilty but they're paid to get them off. I do not think I could let a guilty person be free.

We all walked away that day with a sour taste in our mouths. I was asked a couple of weeks later what I thought. I told the newspaper that changes needed to be made to avoided the intimidation of jurors in high-profile cases. I believe we need a system like the court of appeals with a panel of three judges. That would be fairer and more independent. I told the paper that even if jurors were not physically threatened or intimidated, there was a real underlying fear because of the reputation of bikies and high-profile criminals. If we had a system with three judges sitting on these sorts of murder cases, they couldn't be manipulated or intimidated.

Attorney General Carl Piot said the idea of eliminating jury trials from high-profile cases involving bikies and crime figures was problematic. He also said threatening or intimidating a juror was a serious offence. As this was the end of the road as far as us going to court, there was relief that it was over, but sadness at the result. With all the bad publicity over all these years, the papers and TV forgot that my brother was still loved by a family. He was still someone's son. He was someone's father, someone's partner, someone's friend. But most of all, he was still my brother.

I was asked to prepare a victim's impact statement at the start of the first trial, but I never got to read it because we had two hung juries and one trial dismissed. This is what I would have said:

> The late James Jobson was my brother. I was asked to do this statement, but finding words to describe a grief I have never felt before is the hardest thing I have ever done. My brother's murder has impacted my family beyond

belief. A sadness that never ends, a grief so overwhelming at times I cannot breathe.

In 2004, our lives changed forever. I was told of my brother's death on the phone at 6:10 a.m. by the police. I had rung to find out if it was my brother who had been killed. Being told over the phone that it was my brother was the cruellest thing. I had been told, as my brother has two little boys and I did not want them to go to school and be told.

From the moment I was told, my life collapsed. I lay in a heap on the floor, sobbing uncontrollably as my two young children watched in horror as their mother was totally inconsolable and not knowing what was wrong. Words could not come from me, as I was in total shock, my body shaking. I had no voice, my heart breaking with every moment that passed. With my brothers' boys I had to be.

As I stood at their front door and their mother opened it, I was in total shock. There were no words that would come. She asked me what the hell was wrong. My grief and despair were apparent. I uttered the words that my brother was dead. I stood there as two boys were told of this horror. The pain and anguish in my brother's eldest child's face will haunt me forever. Their boy was devastated as his mother comforted him. I felt numb. The pain was too much to describe.

As I faced my mother, I saw her in pain that no words can ever describe. My whole body and mind was in overdrive. I was standing in front of my mum and just could not speak the pain was indescribable.

My brother and I had survived a childhood from hell. We found strength in each other to survive. We had a silent truth that we spoke as you had to live it to understand. I have lost my only brother, my other half. When James died, half of me died too. He was part of me that I will never have again. We were part of the same. There is not a day that goes by that he is not in my thoughts. My life has been a living hell.

My mother has died a little each day. She has this guilt that she could not help him There was no help. James had no defence, no hope, and no help. We were not there to help him. We lost the right to be with him at that moment. He took that away from us. I will not tell you my brother was a saint, because he was not, but he was my brother and I loved him with all my heart. I see my mum dying this slow death, and I cannot stop it. I have so much pain in me that I just cannot feel for anyone else. This is my terrible anguish.

My children have lost their uncle He is gone thanks to the person who thought he had the right to take his life. How do I feel? I feel angry and empty. My sadness, it seems, will never go. The healing they say comes with time. It just does not feel possible. How do you put back lives that have been shattered? How do you get back what has been taken, time lost and spent in grief?

I believe that my life will never be the same. I am a very religious person, and I believe in God. I have to believe that I will see James again and this cannot be the end. If asked what punishment should be given to this person, I would request the death penalty, but we do not have it, then life in prison would be right. To think that the person responsible for my brother's death could ever be released would be putting salt into an open wound. He does not deserve to ever see a sunrise or sunset as a free man. If you think I am being bitter, this cannot be helped, and I make no apology for my grief.

Since the truth never came out in court, I'll tell you my theory of the murder. I do believe Tony did it, but I think he was given no choice. The Devil's Dogs hated him so much for what he did, and they were angry at my brother for helping him. I think Tony was ordered to the clubhouse and told to shoot my brother to make up for the rape. The club felt betrayed by my brother. They believed he should have had nothing more to do with Tony. They hated Tony, and he was scared of them. He was pushed and took the coward's way out. Yes, my brother did take him to the clubhouse to be beaten. But James had no other choice. Did Tony get his revenge on a man who risked all to save him? I told my brother this would come back and bite him on the arse, and it did. It cost him his life. I could be wrong, but this is my theory.

My brother once said to me, "There are very few innocent men in prison, but boy there are a lot of guilty men walking our streets."

*Every man's life ends the same way. It's only the details*
*of how he lived and how he died that distinguish one*
*man from another.—Ernest Hemingway*

# CONCLUSION

This is my story. As I finish writing it, I feel a sense of balance come into my life. Not for a very long time have I had it.

It has taken me nine years to finish my book. There have been so many distractions along the way. A murder, three trials, moving, travelling, marrying. I ask myself the question, "When did I stop mourning my brother?" I did not. I still weep. There is a void in my life that will never be filled. So my time of grieving will always be.

I hope you find my story empowering. The times spent in darkness and chaos have reached the end. You might ask, "Do you ever really recover from trauma?" I cannot answer for anyone but myself. I think we learn to understand that we did not cause these horrible things that have happened to us along our journey. Being able to look at yourself in the mirror and actually like the person you see was a major step for me. It was at that moment I knew I would be okay.

My life now and for some years has been on an upward swing. I have the two most amazing children, and I love them more than life itself. I have a husband I adore, and he is the most patient man I have ever met. Like me, my family has gone through these terrible chapters and come out the other side stronger. My work has been amazing. I am fortunate to love my job. It allows me to help and empower young people whose lives somehow slide along where mine has been. There is nothing that a child can tell me that I have not experienced. It is with that knowledge and hope and faith that I can honestly tell them that it will be okay and that they will make it through their dark time.

It is through terrible darkness that we look for the light. I believe that as my soul was being destroyed, it was God who gave me the strength to hold on. When the time was right, he found me. He empowered me to be the best person I could be. I have conviction, I am assertive, and I believe *Changing Chapters* will give hope to people. We are all given different chapters, but we can change pages and learn to move forward. A new page offers new hope

Where we are now:
- Clara Jobson: married, youth worker, mother
- Jenny: married, running a business
- Maria: still practicing law
- Natalie: carer for her children
- Sambo: retired and running a strip place
- Milo Calabrese: in prison
- Tony Frankino: walking the streets a free man

*I may not have gone where I intended to go, but I think I have ended up where I need to be.—Douglas Adams*